Dedications

For

My parents, Naranjan Singh and Mohinder Kaur Johal, who guided me.

My wife Bonny, who keeps me grounded.

My son Amman, who makes me feel proud.

Rat Race
To Riches

Rat Race
To Riches

A ROADMAP TO FINANCIAL
FREEDOM

AKWAL S. JOHAL
FCCA MBA BCOM

Published by Akwal S. Johal.

Paperback ISBN: 979-8-34455-051-0
Hardcover ISBN: 979-8-34455-270-5

Disclaimer and Exclusion of Liability
This book is for general and educational information and use. In particular, the information does not constitute any form of advice, legal, financial, or otherwise, or recommendation and is not intended to be relied upon by users in making or refraining from making any financial or investment decisions. Appropriate independent advice should be obtained before making any such decision.

Whilst every effort has been made to ensure the information in this book is accurate, no liability can be accepted by the author for any loss incurred in any way whatsoever by any person acting or refraining from acting as a result of reading material in this book.

The author makes no guarantee of financial results obtained by using this book.

Visit our website: ratrace2riches.com

CONTENTS

Introduction

*It's not where you start, but
the distance you travel that matters.*

Financial freedom is a lifestyle choice. You choose how you want to spend your time, which is one of your most valuable resources. You can leave your job and live the life you want without having to worry about your next paycheck. You can choose the things you want to buy without feeling constrained by money. Financial freedom gives you the ability to live life on your terms.

All this is possible because you have managed your finances for the lifestyle you want.

In this book, I will share my journey to financial freedom as a roadmap for those who are living paycheck to paycheck and are ready to transform their financial future.

'We came to this country with nothing but five pounds in our pocket!'

My parents arrived in the UK from India in the early 1950s, searching for a better life. They brought up three children, all born in London, who they had educated, married off, and helped to buy their first homes.

Dad was educated up to high school level; he was a fiercely independent man with a strong work ethic. He was guided by the three pillars of his faith: honest hard work, meditation, and sharing with others. He wanted us to grow up to be independent citizens who were self-reliant and not a burden to others.

On the other hand, Mum never went to school, so she could not read or write, but she had a great sense of humour, common sense in abundance and was financially savvy.

Growing up, we spoke Punjabi at home and English at school. Both Mum and Dad worked hard all their lives; they did not have much money, but they both worked and saved so that their children could have a better life.

When I was very young, I would open my Mum's purse and stack the coins in neat bundles, count them, and proudly tell her how much cash she had in her purse. During the summer holidays, we would have friends over and play Monopoly all day. I loved being the banker, buying properties, seeing the cash pile up, and winning. I do not know if this fascination was something I was born with or something I developed. But I do know I had this underlying desire to be independently wealthy from an early age.

Growing up, we were poor. We shared a small, terraced house with two other families. We slept in one room containing three double beds. I remember not having a telephone at home. If my parents needed to call India or a relative in the UK, they would have to go to a friend's house and call from there and pay for the call afterwards. On one occasion, a close relative passed away in the UK, and my parents did not know about it as there was no way of contacting us. Our neighbours passed the message on, and my parents called them back from the neighbour's home. Mum and Dad must have spent hours on our neighbour's phone that night.

I also remember having a black and white television well after our friends had moved onto colour, and they would constantly tease us.

Dad rode a bicycle to work as we never owned a family car. We would always visit our family and friends using public transport, catching the coach, train or bus everywhere.

I am sure my parents would have wanted to own a home telephone, a colour television, and a car but could not afford them. Eventually, we got them, but it was paid for outright with their own money, which they had saved and set aside. By the way, Dad never got his car; he waited for me to grow up, take lessons, and buy the first family car!

One of the other little things that stuck in my mind was my school blazer, which was bought in a jumble sale for 50p. My school blazer was a second-hand navy-coloured jacket, which Mum bought for me out of her hard-earned money. I loved my new blazer and was so proud to wear it to school. But when I got to school, the kids teased me about it, as it turned out to be a boiler suit, and I felt quite embarrassed, but I carried on wearing it.

The journey to financial freedom begins with an underlying desire.

Whatever your reason, the journey to becoming financially free begins with an underlying desire. Your motive may be wanting to escape poverty or never wanting to be pushed around in life. It may be wanting to be financially secure, or you may have developed a taste for some of the finer things in life. Whatever your reason is, it begins with an underlying desire.

My first big lesson on money came at the age of fourteen. I belonged to a small gang of kids growing up, and now and then, we would get ourselves in trouble with the police. Nothing too serious, just silly kids' stuff, being in the wrong place at the wrong time, and mixing with the wrong people. On one occasion, my Mum had to sign me out from the local police station. The next day, two police officers came to our family home and sat with me and my parents. They told me I had a juvenile record and if I did not change my way, I would end up in Borstal, a kind of detention centre used to reform young offenders. This had a profound effect on me.

On Monday morning after assembly, the headmaster called me to his office. He made it clear that either I get an education, which would lead to a good job, or end up in Borstal with a criminal record and struggle to find good work if I was to make one more mistake. I needed that shock to the system. It was a huge wake-up call. I was at a crossroads; I saw clearly that education was a way out of poverty for me.

I had learned my first lesson on money.

Education is a route out of poverty for many people.

From that point onwards, l put my head down and buried it in my books. Education was a way out of poverty, but it was also an escape from all the distractions around me. I studied incredibly hard, and my nickname at school became 'Swot,' finally, all that hard work and sacrifice paid off with a place at university, and being the first person in my family to go to university.

My parents did not have the exposure to offer me any educational or career advice. Back then, the classic parental advice would have been to study hard to become a doctor or engineer, as these were the best-paid and most prestigious jobs around.

Mum wanted us all to study and get good jobs so that we would never get 'pushed around' in life. That was the extent of the career guidance we got. From fifteen, I had to make my own choices when deciding which subjects to study and which career path to take. I did not follow my friends into the sciences: physics, chemistry, and biology to become a doctor or engineer. I followed what felt right to me: a finance and business studies education.

At eighteen, most kids don't know what career they want to pursue. There are a few lucky ones who know exactly what they want to do when they grow up, but they are in the minority. One such person was a close friend at school whose parents owned their own business. I asked my friend what he was going to do after leaving school. He said he wanted to become an accountant as they earned good money. I carried out my own research and decided that this was what I wanted to do as I was good at maths and wanted to be independently wealthy. For me, it was that simple: I chose to study commerce at the University of Birmingham as a route into accountancy.

I was never naturally academic. I had to work hard and persevere to make up for it. I graduated from university with a Bachelor of Commerce degree, after which I qualified as a Chartered Certified Accountant and later was sponsored by my employer to study for an MBA at Henley Business School.

I remember thinking when I qualified as an Accountant in my twenties that, I would not have to struggle like my parents. I would always have a secure job and would never be unemployed, but I found out not long after that this was naive.

My strong work ethic came from my parents. Dad worked nights at the bakery and slept during the daytime. He believed in honest hard work and would often say, 'Whatever job you do, try to do the best you can.' Mum worked in the laundry department at the local hospital and juggled her time between work, home, and raising three kids.

I had a lot of part-time jobs growing up. I started delivering newspapers at the age of twelve. I worked in Petticoat Lane market selling sweatshirts at fifteen, and at the weekends, I would work in a corner shop stacking shelves. During my summer holidays, I took jobs selling suits at Marks & Spencer, working nights baking bread at our local bakery, working on market stalls during university, and so on. It was great having my own money. I contributed towards the household bills as I knew my parents would never accept a penny in rent from me living at home. Having part-time jobs gave me an appreciation of how hard my parents worked, how much they sacrificed to give their children a good life, and an appreciation for the value of money.

Both my parents and teachers advised me to study and get a well-paid, secure job. This mantra was drilled into me. But life is not a straight line. There are ups and downs, and life was about to teach me another valuable lesson.

I left university to work for Peat Marwick McLintock, now known as KPMG, one of the top accountancy firms in the world. After a few years, I moved into the banking sector in London's financial district, known as 'The Square Mile.' Before long, I was married, owned our first home, and had a baby on the way. Just as life was getting good, a deep recession hit!

The second biggest money lesson came when I was thirty years old. It was a cold Friday morning in November 1992. I will remember this day for the rest of my life. Quite literally, one moment, I had a promising career at Standard Chartered Bank, and then the next, I was jobless on the street.

It was brutal, like any other Friday morning I was on my computer at 9 a.m. ready to start the day, when I and a few work colleagues were summoned into the Finance Director's office. He was standing there with the Head of Human Resources, and by 9:30 a.m., I was on the street.

This was my light-bulb moment, a moment of clarity, a realisation that I no longer wanted to be at the mercy of anyone. I realised I wanted to be financially secure and independent; I wanted financial freedom.

Your darkest hour can transform an underlying desire into a burning desire.

It was a shocking and humiliating experience. I was escorted by a security guard back to my desk. I switched off my computer, put on my coat, collected my personal belongings, handed back my security card, and was frog-marched off the premises like a common thief. And all this in front of my closest friends and work colleagues. They did not look up or say goodbye as they were all shocked and afraid of what was happening.

Most of the staff who lost their jobs that day went to the pub to drink their sorrows away. I probably should have joined them, but all I wanted to do was to see my Mum. I was at my Mum's house by 11 a.m. and was just glad to see her. I felt like a failure and was ashamed to go home that day.

I had learned my second big lesson on money.

An education and a well-paid job don't offer you financial security.

The mantra, go to school and get an education and a well-paid secure job, which was drilled into me at home and school, was now shattered. Being young and having experienced redundancy for the first time, of course, you take it personally. I thought I was not good enough and was a failure in some way. I had never heard of a recession or downsizing before that day and thought my banking job was secure. That may have been the case for my parent's generation, but I learned that job security was a thing of the past. Companies reduce their headcount, especially during a recession, and employees need to expect this to happen to them at least a couple of times during their working lives.

In the back of my head, my biggest fear was that I had a home that was heavily mortgaged, my wife was eight months pregnant and on maternity leave, and I had just lost my job in the middle of a deep recession. The mortgage payments on our home were high, and if I did not keep up with the monthly payments, we would be at risk of losing our home with a baby on the way.

There is an old saying: desperation is a good teacher. I learned that Friday in November 1992, that no job is secure. This is not personal; none of us are indispensable, and there was no loyalty, whatever your length of service.

This was my darkest hour, a life-changing event that would be etched in my mind forever. I vowed never to be at the mercy of an employer again. I now had a *burning desire* for financial freedom. I wanted financial independence from my employer, which meant I did not want to be dependent on a paycheck, and financial security for my family, which meant we could not lose the roof over our heads.

I sometimes get asked the question by close friends and family members, 'What lessons can you give to a young person who wants to become wealthy?' There is no single formula or path to wealth, however, here are some of the ways:

Inherited wealth: You are born into money.

Marrying up: Marry someone who is wealthy or has prospects (and as Warren Buffett says, 'And hope they don't mind marrying down!').

Luck: Do not underestimate the importance luck plays in being successful. Being in the right place, at the right time, to capitalise on a once-in-a-lifetime opportunity happens.

Education: Highly educated professionals like doctors, lawyers, accountants, bankers, IT specialists, scientists, etc., are some of the best-paid jobs in the world. Education gives you a piece of paper, which becomes your 'unique selling point' and provides you with a competitive edge over others. This piece of paper differentiates you from the masses. These highly skilled professions tend to be 'closed shops' as the supply of labour is limited. Their scarcity ensures they are rewarded well and remain well paid.

Hard work: Working longer hours or taking on a second job will increase your earned income. Moreover, if successful, this may result in promotion to a senior position, commanding a higher salary and benefits package.

Business: Owning a successful business is a great way to make money, as every ounce of effort you put in comes back to you in the way of profit. However, not everyone is cut out for running their own business. Businesses are cyclical, and most people like the certainty of a regular income, and there is always the risk of failure.

Outside of the first three, the main routes to becoming wealthy are education, hard work, or owning a successful business. One path is no better than the other; if you are successful, you can become wealthy through any of these paths. Following one or more of these paths can increase your chances of becoming wealthy, but it does not guarantee it.

Moreover, I find it more useful to talk about the key attributes that underpin becoming wealthy. You need to have the ability, desire, and application to do so.

The key attributes to becoming wealthy

Ability: Financial Intelligence

Who's in charge, you or your money? Financial literacy gives you the ability to control and manage your finances.

Financial literacy gives you the ability to make informed decisions and avoid costly mistakes. Unfortunately, the opposite is also true. Financial ignorance can result in poor decision-making and harm your financial health.

Desire: Having a Burning Desire

The catalyst for a burning desire is usually a life-changing event, and in my case, it was losing my job when I was financially vulnerable. This transforms an underlying desire into a burning desire.

Application: Having a Vision and Game Plan

All journeys begin in the mind. A vision is a dream, an idea or a picture in your mind of what the future looks like when you get there, and this can be realised through having a game plan.

I wanted financial security for my family, which meant living debt-free so we could never lose the roof over our heads, and financial independence from my employer, which meant generating sufficient passive income so that we would never be dependent on a paycheck.

> *I believe anyone, regardless of their income level, can become wealthy. Building wealth has more to do with your mindset and behaviour than your ability to earn more income.*

I firmly believe low-income earners can become wealthy. Living on a budget, they understand what it is like to live on very little and, therefore, can develop the drive and determination to build a better life for themselves. Poverty and desperation are good teachers; they can teach us to spend our money frugally, save a higher proportion of our earnings, and invest in building wealth.

We cut back our spending to the essentials and used our savings to stay afloat, knowing we now had another mouth to feed. These should have been the happiest days of my life, but instead became my darkest.

After a difficult period, I got my break and joined Mortgage Express, one of the largest centralised mortgage lenders in the country, part of the Lloyds TSB Banking Group. At Mortgage Express, I saw how mortgage lenders change their strategy to make money throughout each stage of the property cycle. This experience was going to become valuable to me in the future.

I also worked in finance roles in the investment banking sector for several years. I was a Financial Controller at Capstone Mortgages, a subsidiary of Lehman Brothers, an Investment Controller at GE Insurance Holdings, part of GE Capital, and a Global IT Controller at Dresdner Kleinwort Benson, where I had direct access to the trading floors. During this time, I saw the importance of data in making investment decisions, an approach called fundamental analysis.

From what I observed in these two distinct sectors, property and investment banking, I developed my strategy by adapting the investment approach from financial markets to the property sector. I call this the *Property Cycle Investment Strategy*, a strategy based on fundamental analysis and underpinned by sound economic theory. If experienced professional traders were making investment decisions based on data, then this is something I could apply to the property market.

Slowly but surely, I began to develop my passive income outside of my full-time job, which eventually enabled me to achieve the financial freedom I desired. It is important to do things at your own pace. I am a big believer in, *'Slow and steady wins the race.'* You must balance your needs, your family, your work, your health, and your finances. All journeys take time, and the journey to financial freedom cannot be achieved overnight.

In 1993, we were on a knife edge. I was jobless in the middle of a deep recession. My wife was on maternity leave, we had a newborn baby, and on top of all that, we had a large mortgage to pay. If we had not kept up with our mortgage payments, we would have lost our home. By 2005, we had moved into our dream home, paid off our mortgage, and created a passive income that exceeded our expenses. In 12 years, we went from financial vulnerability to becoming financially independent. Most of this was achieved not from higher earned income but from having a vision, sticking to a plan, persevering, and believing in yourself.

This book is aimed at those who feel trapped in the rat race, working hard with no time to spare to do the things they enjoy. Their job offers them very little financial security, and they live paycheck to paycheck. If you want to escape the rat race and transform your financial future, this book offers you a guide on how this can be achieved. Reading about my lived experience may inspire others to find their own path.

To help share my experience, I have developed the *Cashflow Model* and *Financial Freedom Matrix*.

The Cashflow Model helps us to understand how money comes in and goes out. Using the Cashflow Model, we will see how low and middle-income families make their money compared to the wealthy. We will see clearly that these groups make their money in completely different ways and what needs to be done to become independently wealthy.

The Financial Freedom Matrix is a timeless roadmap to financial freedom. The roadmap has six milestones, shown below, from which you can develop your own unique plan to help achieve your goals.

The best way to view this diagram is to see it as a continuum with financial dependence at one end and financial freedom at the other.

Six Milestones

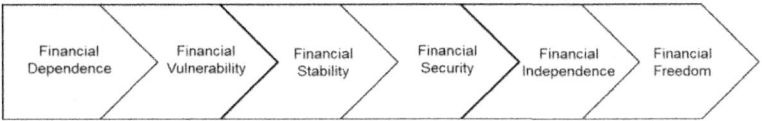

The final destination may have been financial freedom, but in hindsight, I found the real hidden gem was the journey.

The ultimate goal was conquering my self-doubts, fears, negative thoughts, and beginning to believe in myself. It is these insecurities that keep you trapped in the rat race, where you end up playing it safe. I started to trust my instincts and believe in myself.

In hindsight, what was my darkest hour turned out to be the best thing that ever happened to me. Losing my job set me on the path to financial freedom.

Before we can start building wealth, we need to build up our Financial IQ, and that's the subject of the next chapter.

NOTES

CHAPTER 1:
Financial Literacy

The single most important word in finance is cashflow.

*Do not give your children money; give them
something far more important: The knowledge
to make, keep and grow money.*

Aren't you glad we studied Pythagoras's theorem and the formula for solving a quadratic equation at school? Since leaving school, I can count the number of times I have used this knowledge on one hand. The one skill that would have been extremely useful to learn, and I would guarantee most people would use it throughout their lives, managing your money, was never taught.

Managing your money is an essential life skill and should be taught in every school. Without financial literacy you end up having money problems, you struggle with debt and constantly worry about how to make ends meet. Moreover, you make poor financial decisions, let investment opportunities pass you by and in the long run miss out on your dreams. Financial literacy allows you to take back control of your money.

Many young people leave school today not understanding the basics of opening a bank account, spending their money carefully, putting some money aside as savings or investing for their future, yet they are bombarded with offers of credit cards for which they are ill-prepared. Our education system fails to prepare young people for managing their personal finances.

Dad was educated, hard-working and fiercely independent. On the other hand, Mum never went to school but had common sense in abundance and was financially savvy.

Before we start building wealth, we need to build up our financial literacy.

Financial literacy doesn't mean studying for qualifications in business, finance, accounting or investments. What I am referring to is being financially savvy, which is about managing your money in a way that builds wealth. The good news is that anyone can achieve this. You don't need to have a master's degree in finance to apply this knowledge!

I completely understand that finance can be a dry subject for many people, so the challenge for me as a writer is to make finance as interesting as possible. I get that; after all, if I had difficulty sleeping, I would read a page from my auditing book, and that would do the trick! I want this book to entertain you first and foremost, and hopefully, in the process, you will learn something. I think Walt Disney said it best:

'I would rather entertain and hope that people learned something, than educate people and hope they were entertained.'

The most important concept in finance is cashflow. My challenge is to get this across in one chapter in the most interesting way I can. I will demystify much of the financial jargon and explain technical concepts in plain English. I will use my personal experience to make it relatable, and diagrams to visually explain concepts, in the hope that you will want to turn the page and finish reading the book. I believe anyone reading this book will be able to improve their Financial IQ.

***I have yet to meet a wealthy person who is
not good at managing their money.***

If you want to drive a car, you take driving lessons. If you want to ski, you take skiing lessons and so on. Therefore, it makes complete sense that if you want to become wealthy, you need to take finance lessons.

Financially savvy people understand how money works, that is, how money comes in and goes out. Financial literacy can help make you wealthy simply by managing your finances in a way that builds wealth. Conversely, a lack of financial literacy can destroy wealth through ill-informed decision-making, frittering away your earnings and acquiring liabilities.

Studying accountancy in the evenings and weekends while working full-time was tough. It meant coming home after a long day at work and putting in a few hours before bed. Working and studying at the same time also meant staying home at weekends while my friends would be out partying. There were a lot of sacrifices made.

I was newly married and needed to balance my time between home, work and studies. Eventually, it all paid off. I qualified as an accountant in my late twenties and became a member of the Association of Chartered Certified Accountants.

I then went on to study for my MBA at Henley Business School. This was hard work, as I would get to work early every morning for 2 years to spend a couple of hours studying before my working day started. This was a broader business studies course, which helped me think strategically.

Accountancy is the language of money, and the single most important word in accountancy is cashflow. In much the same way, professions like law, medicine, science, engineering, and so on have their own language and vocabulary; the language of money is accountancy.

Cashflow is King.

The best way to illustrate how money works, that is, how money comes in and goes out, is to understand the Cashflow Model. Cashflow refers to the cash flowing into and out of your bank account.

Cashflow is the single most important concept in finance because it combines the two most important financial statements: The Income Statement (also known as the Profit and Loss account) and the Balance Sheet.

Let me explain what I mean. The Income Statement has two components:

INCOME: A transaction that puts **money into** your bank account.

EXPENSE: A transaction that takes **money out** of your bank account.

The Income Statement summarises the INCOME earned and EXPENSES incurred during the reporting period, which is typically a year. If INCOME exceeds EXPENSES, we make a profit. Otherwise, we make a loss. The Income Statement shows us how we have performed over the year, a bit like a movie.

The cashflow pattern for the Income Statement is shown below.

The Income Statement

In the business world, sales revenue would be an example of INCOME and payroll costs would be an example of an EXPENSE.

In the world of personal finance, we look at cash coming in and out of our bank account. If we take the example of an individual who has a job and lives in rented accommodation. Their salary is INCOME as this is *money into* their bank account, and their rent is an EXPENSE as this is *money out* of their bank account.

The second financial statement is the Balance Sheet. Again, this has two components for simplicity:

ASSET: Something you own or are owed that puts **money into** your bank account.

LIABILITY: Something you own or owe that takes **money out** of your bank account.

The Balance Sheet is a summary of all the ASSETS and LIABILITIES we have. As such, the Balance Sheet shows us a snapshot of our financial position at a single point in time, typically the end of the year, a bit like a photograph.

The cashflow pattern for the Balance Sheet is shown below.

The Balance Sheet

In the business world, a debtor is an example of an ASSET, and a business loan is an example of a LIABILITY.

In the world of personal finance, we look at cash coming in and out of our bank account. If we take the example of an individual owning stocks and shares in a quoted company. The stocks and shares are ASSETS as the company pays the shareholder dividend income, putting *money into* their bank account. Let us assume this individual has an outstanding credit card balance. This would be an example of a LIABILITY, as the credit card company charges interest on your outstanding balance, and this takes *money out* of your bank account.

Of course, there are technical accounting definitions for assets and liabilities, but for our purposes, I want to keep it simple. The key is to *follow the money*; simply put, assets put money into your bank account, and liabilities take money out.

Also, when classifying something as an asset or a liability, if the item purchased is funded by a loan, then treat it as one item and do not separate the two components.

The biggest mistake I see people making is believing their home and car are assets. Follow the money; assets put money into your bank account, and liabilities take money out.

The following are examples of assets and liabilities:

Equity: Stocks and shares are assets as they put money into your bank account in the form of dividend income.

Savings: A Savings Account is an asset as it puts money into your bank account in the form of interest income.

Car: A Car you have bought outright is a liability, not an asset, as it takes money out of your bank account in the form of expenses for repairs and maintenance, taxes, insurance, fuel, roadworthiness tests, and servicing costs. To be more precise, a car is a depreciating liability as it falls in value each year.

Buying a car, a depreciating liability funded by a car loan on which you pay interest is one of the biggest mistakes I see young people make. I can understand why young people want a prestigious car in their 20s and 30s, but this is one of the biggest wealth destroyers.

This is because it is a triple whammy. Firstly, you are taking on debt. Secondly, you pay the finance company interest on the car loan, and thirdly, the car depreciates, so you will never get back what you paid. This is one of the fastest ways to destroy wealth and become poorer.

Short-term debt: Payday loans, credit cards, store cards, personal loans, overdrafts and 0% finance are liabilities because they take money out of your bank account in the form of interest expense and fees.

Short-term debts are wealth killers because if you cannot pay off the balance in full, as and when due, the interest rate and fees charged are extremely high.

Home: A home is a liability.

To be more precise, a home is a necessary liability, as we all need somewhere to live.

Buying a home to live in is a liability, not an asset, because it takes money out of your bank account. There are expenses in the form of mortgage interest, building and contents insurance, utilities, repairs and maintenance to pay.

Even after the mortgage has been fully paid off, the home remains a liability as it still takes money out of your bank account.

Buying a home beyond your means is another wealth killer. Not only do you have to pay the mortgage, but the running costs, repairs, and maintenance can be quite substantial on a large property.

Contrary to what many people think, a home is not an asset. Any appreciation in value is an unrealised gain and, therefore, should be ignored from a cashflow perspective until it is realised. The way to realise any appreciation is to sell or re-mortgage. The problem with selling is that you still need somewhere to live. And, if you re-mortgage, you will now have acquired a liability on which you have to pay interest and repay the capital.

Rental Property: A rental property can be an asset or a liability, depending on whether it is making money or losing money.

If the rental property is making money by generating a positive cashflow, it is an asset. If the rental property is losing money by generating a negative cashflow, it is a liability. Do not separate the property from the loan. Treat them as one item for the purpose of this classification. Keep it simple.

The real magic happens when you merge the Income Statement and the Balance Sheet with the bank account at its intersection. You get the Cashflow Model. The income statement is along the horizontal axis, and the balance sheet is on the vertical axis, both generate cash inflows and outflows with the bank account at the centre. The arrows show the flow of cash. The Cashflow Model captures all cash movements flowing in and out of the bank account over the course of the reporting period, typically a year. It shows where money comes in from, the sources of cash, and where it goes out, the uses of cash.

The Cashflow Model

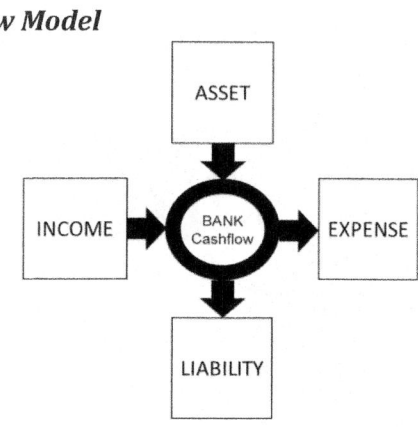

Cash inflows are:

INCOME: A transaction that puts **money into** your bank account.

ASSET: Something you own or are owed that puts **money into** your bank account.

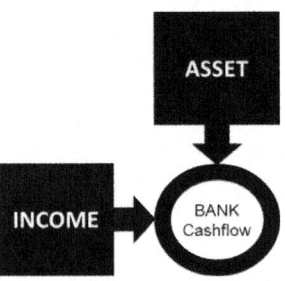

It then follows that the way to make money is by having a well-paid job, a profitable business or by acquiring income-generating assets.

Cash outflows are:

EXPENSE: A transaction that takes **money out** of your bank account.

LIABILITY: Something you own or owe that takes **money out** of your bank account.

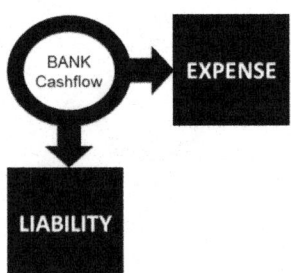

It then follows that the way you lose money is through uncontrolled expenditure and by taking on excessive liabilities.

Cashflow is king. This is the single most important financial concept you need to understand to take control of your finances and build wealth. Good cashflow management creates wealth, and poor cashflow management destroys wealth.

At its most basic level, the way to build wealth is to have more money coming in than going out.

The term cashflow refers to the net amount of cash flowing in and out of the bank account. Therefore, cashflow can be positive or negative. A positive cashflow arises when the cash flowing in exceeds the cash flowing out of the bank account. Conversely, a negative cashflow arises when the cash flowing out exceeds the cash flowing in.

A negative cashflow might not be a problem in the short term as it can be covered by dipping into savings, selling assets or borrowing. However, it may indicate an underlying problem. If a negative cashflow persists in the long term, it could develop into a major problem.

Now, let's take a look at the cashflow pattern for low and middle-income families and compare them to the wealthy.

Cashflow pattern for low-income families

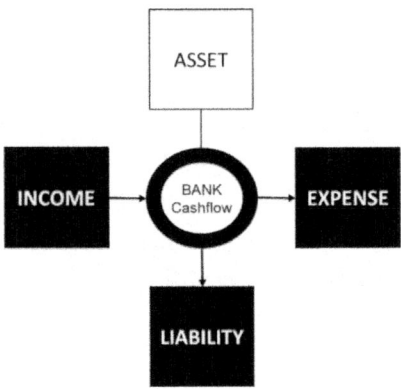

Low-income families make their money principally by exchanging their time for money along the horizontal axis, and they supplement this with short-term debt. Many low-income families live paycheck to paycheck.

To illustrate, a low-income person receives wages as INCOME, and with that, they pay for their EXPENSES such as rent, food and bills. From time to time, they supplement their lifestyle with short-term debt, such as credit cards, which are LIABILITIES.

Cashflow pattern for middle-income families

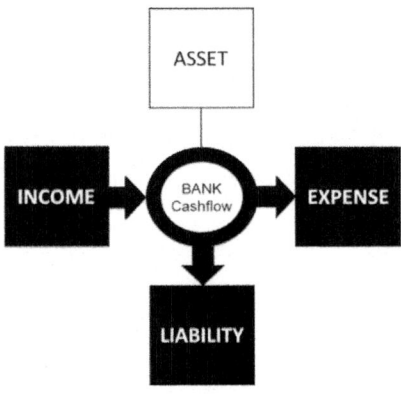

Equally, many middle-income families live paycheck to paycheck.

To illustrate, a middle-income person receives a good salary as INCOME, and with that, they pay for their EXPENSES such as household bills, the cost of running a car, private school fees and holidays. They buy a home that is mortgaged and expensive to maintain; this is a LIABILITY as it takes money out of their bank account. As their incomes rise, so do their expenses. This is called lifestyle inflation.

The rat race is described as a cycle where you wake up, go to work, pay the bills, and go to bed... the next day, you wake up, and the cycle continues. This is the rat race, an endless, self-defeating, pointless pursuit. Whatever money comes in goes out again, and by the end of the month, you have nothing to show for all your hard work. You feel like you are working hard only to make your employer, the government, the banks, and the landlord rich!

There are many people who are 'just about managing,' and if they were to lose their job, they would not last three months without having to borrow money. They are financially vulnerable, and the main reason for this is poor cashflow management. Consequently, many low and middle-income families live paycheck to paycheck.

Generally, the wealthy don't work for money; money works for them. The wealthy make their money from the asset side of the balance sheet, along the vertical axis. That is, they acquire assets which work for them. Each asset is like an employee for the wealthy, who works 24 hours a day, 7 days a week, 365 days a year and does not get sick or take holidays.

Cashflow pattern for the Wealthy

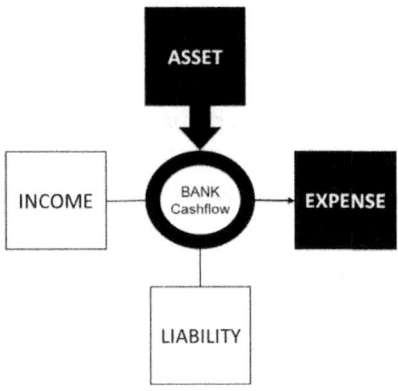

This means that while the wealthy are asleep, their money is still working for them.

Many low and middle-income families are just about managing to stay afloat. Their cashflow pattern shows whatever money comes into the bank as earned income goes back out again in the form of expenses and debt interest. This is a poor cashflow pattern; cash leaks out in the form of expenses and liabilities.

On the other hand, the cashflow pattern for the wealthy shows they have assets that generate a passive income in the form of interest, capital gains, dividends, rental income, and so on, which exceeds their expenses, and any surplus is then re-invested to buy more assets, so their wealth continues to grow. This is a good cashflow pattern. Cash flows out to pay expenses, which are controlled, and any surplus is re-invested back into buying more income-generating assets.

Low and middle-income families make their money
along the horizontal line, the income statement.
On the other hand, the wealthy make their money
from the vertical line, the balance sheet.

We can clearly see that low and middle-income families make their money in a completely different way from that of the wealthy. The analogy I like to use is that low and middle-income families work the land for money. By contrast, the wealthy make their money by planting seeds, which grow into large trees over time, and in the future, they enjoy their fruit and sit under their shade.

This comparison is useful because it shows us that for low and middle-income families to become wealthy, they need to spend their earned income frugally, pay off any debts, set aside any surplus cash as savings, and then begin buying income-generating assets.

'When the tide goes out, we will soon see who has been
swimming in the nude.' - Warren Buffett

The next concept I want to discuss is the distinction between being rich and being wealthy.

Rich is external; it is what you can see, whereas wealth is internal; it is invisible.

Someone with a big house and a luxury car, who wears designer clothes and whose social media profile portrays a lavish lifestyle, is most likely rich. Irrespective of how they have funded their lifestyle, whether they pay for it with cash or debt, they need a certain level of income to support this lifestyle. Their money is tied up in visible possessions.

Someone wealthy is harder to spot because their wealth is invisible. We don't see their savings accounts, investments in the stock market, bonds and pension funds. They forgo current expenditure for greater returns in the future. Their money is tied up in invisible income-generating assets, which provide a reliable and sustainable passive income source for the long term.

Rich people earn a good income, but as their incomes rise, so do their expenses and liabilities. They spend money on possessions that bring them prestige. Their lifestyle is high-end. They spend money to enjoy their money, and in the process, they believe they gain respect and admiration for their achievements.

Wealthy people, on the other hand, spend their money on income-generating and appreciating assets. They live below their means. They resist the temptation of an immediate reward in favour of a more valuable reward in the future, a concept called delayed gratification.

So, the next time you are walking down the street and see a person dressed up or dressed down, don't be too quick to judge. The world is full of people who look ordinary yet wealthy and others who look rich yet are living on a knife edge and are just one paycheck away from going bust.

In the animal kingdom, the rich are like peacocks who love to show off their beautiful feathers to gain the admiration of others. This reminds me of a story I once heard.

A peacock was standing in a field chatting with a bull. 'When I was younger, I used to be able to fly to the top of that tree in one go. I would love to get to the top of that tree, just one more time,' sighed the peacock, 'but I don't have the strength anymore.'

'Well, why don't you nibble on some of my droppings?' replied the bull. 'They're packed with nutrients.'

The peacock pecked at some dung and found that it gave him enough strength to reach the first branch of the tree. The next day, after eating some more dung, he reached the second branch. And similarly for the third day. Finally, on the fourth day, he was proudly perched at the top of the tree.

It was then that a farmer from a nearby field saw the peacock; he dashed into the farmhouse, emerged with a shotgun, and shot the peacock right out of the tree.

The moral of the story is bullshit might get you to the top, but it won't keep you there!

A rich lifestyle funded by excessive debt is not sustainable in the long term; at some point, you will have to pay it back; otherwise, it will bring you down to earth with a bump.

So, how do you measure financial wealth?

Definition of Financial Wealth

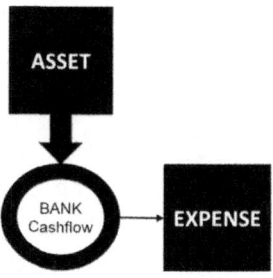

My preferred definition of financial wealth is debt-free and having a passive income that exceeds your expenses.

You are independently wealthy when you live debt-free
and your passive income > expenses, or simply put,
you don't owe anyone money and you make
more money than you spend.

If you only looked at passive income exceeding your expenses as a measure of wealth, then this would only give you half the picture. To become independently wealthy, you need to be both debt-free and have a passive income that exceeds your expenses. That is, you need to look at both parts of the cashflow model: the balance sheet and the income statement.

A good measure of financial wealth is the number of times your passive income covers your expenses. For instance, 2x means your passive income is double your expenses, 3x means your passive income is triple your expenses and so on.

Before we move on to building wealth, let's take a quick peek at the main things that destroy wealth:

Poor financial literacy
Short-term high-interest debt
Buying a car on finance
Buying a home that is beyond your means
Going cheap
Investing without a game plan
Yourself

These are the big-ticket items which destroy wealth. Forget saving a few pennies here and there on coffees and take-outs; these big-ticket items have the largest impact on destroying wealth, and we will cover them in more detail later.

Next, let's discover how to build wealth using the financial freedom matrix.

NOTES

CHAPTER 2:

Financial Freedom Matrix

'The path is the goal.' - Mahatma Gandhi

'A journey of a thousand miles begins with a single step.'
- Lao Tzu

W e live in a world of 'celebrity culture' where we are constantly exposed to the personal lives of our music, media and sporting idols. We see our idols and the lifestyles they lead and want it for ourselves. Not just that, we want it instantly, at the click of an app, and without having to do any of the hard work.

What the public rarely sees is all the hard work and sacrifice it takes to get there.

Boxer Mike Tyson had 24 first-round knock-outs during his career, earning him the name 'Iron Mike.' During his career, he earned, on average, $7.5 million per fight in winnings.[1] Many people watched and thought, 'Not bad money for three minutes of work.' This is what people see, but what they don't see is the weeks, months, and years of dedication, sacrifice, and training Mike Tyson put in, not only to get to the top of his game but to stay there.

There are no shortcuts to success, but it is achievable for anyone prepared to work for it.

To achieve financial freedom, you need to create a passive income stream that is reliable and sustainable for the long term. You are not interested in one-off or short-term successes as these are not repeatable. It takes time to build wealth, but once you achieve your goal, the rewards are worth the effort.

Financial Freedom is the pinnacle of wealth.

Having control over your time and the freedom of choice to do what you want, when you want, for as long as you want, is the ultimate currency.

To help explain the journey, I designed the Financial Freedom Matrix, which is a roadmap to financial freedom. The typical path is shown by the arrow, which travels through all four stages – the learner, the rat race, the investor and finally, the financial freedom stage.

Along the horizontal axis, we have ASSETS split into low and high, denoting asset poor and asset rich, respectively. Similarly, along the vertical axis, we have TIME split into low and high, denoting time poor and time rich, respectively.

Financial Freedom Matrix

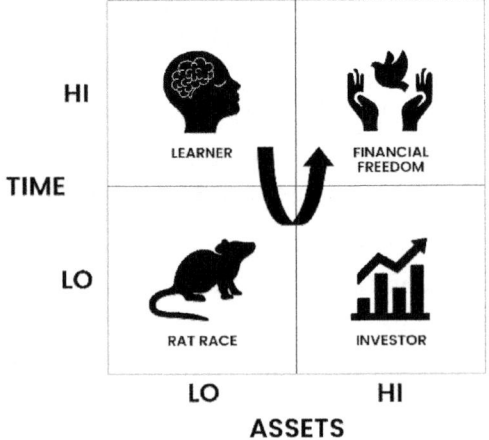

Each stage has corresponding milestones, as shown below, from which you can develop a plan to help achieve your goal.

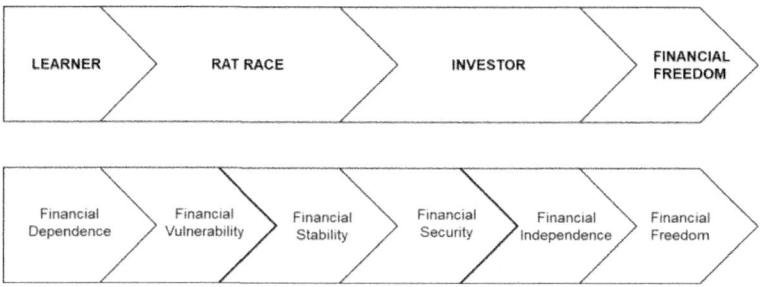

There are four distinct stages:

The Learner Stage

Stage 1: The Learner is categorised as Asset Poor-Time Rich.

Typically, this would be an 18-year-old student living at home and working part-time.

We learn by absorbing information from our environment, life experiences, and school. These formative years are important as they shape the person we become.

Financial Dependence describes a situation where you depend on your parents for essentials like food, clothes and a roof over your head.

The Rat Race Stage

Stage 2: The Rat Race is categorised as Asset Poor-Time Poor.

Typically, you will have completed your formal education and are now working or running your own business.

You wake up, go to work, pay the bills, and go to bed ... the next day, you wake up, and the cycle continues. This is the rat race, an endless, self-defeating, pointless pursuit. Whatever money comes in goes out again, and by the end of the month, you have nothing to show for all your hard work. You feel like you are working hard only to make your employer, the government, the banks, and the landlord rich!

This is potentially one of the longest stages, ranging from 20 to 65 years old. Most people remain trapped in the rat race until they retire in their mid-60s unless they have a plan B, a backup plan.

During the rat race stage, you move from Financial Vulnerability to Financial Stability. This can be achieved by increasing your income, and perhaps more significantly for most people, by changing your behaviour.

The Investor Stage

Stage 3: The Investor is categorised as Asset Rich - Time Poor.

Typically, you are in full-time employment, developing your side hustles, striving to live debt-free and generating a passive income stream by acquiring assets. Over time, your passive income will grow and become a greater proportion of your total income. You are growing less and less dependent on your paycheck.

During the investor stage, you are moving from:

Financial Stability to Financial Security by living debt-free, and from

Financial Security to Financial Independence by buying income-generating assets.

The Financial Freedom Stage

Stage 4: Financial Freedom is categorised as Asset Rich - Time Rich.

You chose to quit your job.

Financial Freedom is a lifestyle choice. You choose how you want to spend your time, which is one of your most valuable resources. You can leave your job and live the life you want without having to worry about your next paycheck. You can choose the things you want to buy without feeling constrained by money. Financial freedom gives you the ability to live life on your terms.

All this is possible because you have managed your finances for the lifestyle you want.

Financial freedom lives at the top of the mountain, and there are many paths to get there. This is because everyone's character, environment, and financial circumstances are different. Everyone's path is unique.

The path is the goal. Listen to your heart, your mind, your body, and your soul, and they will reveal your passion. What grabs your attention, makes you happy, and lifts your soul? Look for the answer within, and this will guide you on your path.

Dad was deeply spiritual and would tell me that we are all looking outside ourselves, and we forget the power that lies within. If you listen to your inner voice and trust your gut instinct, it will point you towards your path. Everything we need to succeed is contained within; we just need to believe in ourselves.

I found working for other people challenging, especially poor management. I had a good job; it paid the bills and put food on the table, but deep down, I wanted to follow my passion. I needed to work for money to pay the bills; the job became a means to an end. Internally, my heart, mind, body and soul, in fact, every fibre of my body, was screaming at me to get out and follow my path.

My passion has always been property. That's what gets me excited. So, I had to find a way to work to pay the bills and, in parallel, build up my own rental income stream. That was my path.

Stop trying to be the person you think everyone expects you to be. Be yourself because everyone else is taken!

Stop looking externally and copying other people. Find your path by looking internally and following it. Follow *your* path, and focus on what *you* want to achieve in *your* timescale, taking account of *your* risk appetite.

Real growth comes from the journey and the lessons learned from facing our challenges and conquering our self-doubts.

In many ways, the journey is more important than the final destination. You will face challenges and make mistakes along the way; overcoming them will shape the person you become. See every challenge along the way as an opportunity to learn, develop, and grow. It is during these difficult times that we truly experience growth and discover who we really are.

The final destination may be financial freedom, but in hindsight, I found the real hidden gem was the journey. I began to believe in myself, I overcame my self-doubts, and I began to trust myself.

What was my darkest hour, losing my job with a baby on the way and a mortgage to pay, in hindsight, was the best thing to happen to me as I found my path. It is only by facing our challenges and conquering our self-doubts that we truly grow. I learned that security does not lie in having things but in knowing how to handle things.

Believe in yourself.

Also, it is only by facing your challenges that you conquer your self-doubts, fears and negative thoughts. It is these insecurities that keep you trapped in the rat race where you seek financial security. This is not all that surprising as we have been taught to go to school and get a secure job, whereas the reality is that this traps you in a rat race which offers very little financial security.

The Financial Freedom Matrix shows the typical four stages in the journey. Of course, these four stages are not mutually exclusive. You can have your feet in more than one stage at any one point. For instance, you could straddle the investor and financial freedom stage if you decide you want to work part-time and, on your days off, pursue your hobbies and interests.

Born into money, Marrying-up and Luck

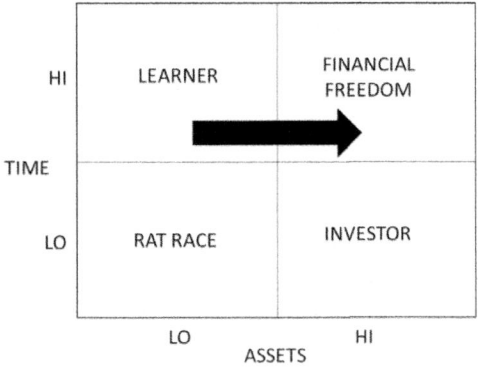

Similarly, these four stages are not sequential. You can go from learner directly to the financial freedom stage if you are born into money, marry up or are lucky enough to win the lottery. It is possible to leap-frog the journey; however, these scenarios are fairly rare.

To determine which milestone you have reached in your journey, we need to look at 5 Key Performance Indicators (KPIs):

1. Cashflow: Do you have a positive cashflow? A positive cashflow builds wealth because you have more money coming in than going out.

2. Savings Cover: How many months of expenses have been set aside as savings? This measures the size of our emergency buffer, our cushion against short-term cashflow shocks arising from unexpected bills or a loss of income.

3. Short-Term Debt: Have you cleared all your short-term debt? This measures our dependency on bad debt.

4. Debt Free: Are you living debt-free? This measures what we owe.

5. Passive Income > Expenses: Does your passive income exceed your expenses? This is a measure of financial wealth.

You are independently wealthy when you meet all 5 KPIs.

The table below summarises the relationship between the 5 KPIs and the milestones, and by completing the 360 Cashflow Statement, you can determine which milestone you have reached. Note that the milestones are sequential. That is, you cannot move to the next milestone without the criteria for the preceding ones being complete.

KPI/Milestone table

#	KPI's	Criteria	Learner	Rat Race		Investor		Financial Freedom
			Financial Dependence	Financial Vulnerability	Financial Stability	Financial Security	Financial Independence	Financial Freedom
1	Cashflow	Do you have a positive cashflow ?	N/A	N	Y	Y	Y	Y
2	Savings Cover	How many months of expenses have been set aside as savings ?	N/A	< 3	3 +	6 +	12 +	12-36
3	Short-Term Debt	Have you cleared all your Short-Term Debt ?	N/A	N	Y	Y	Y	Y
4	Debt Free	Are you living debt free ?	N/A	N	N	Y	Y	Y
5	PI > EXP	Does your passive income exceed your expenses ?	N/A	N	N	N	Y	Y

Now, let's take a deep dive into the four stages to financial freedom.

NOTES

CHAPTER 2.1:

The Learner

Invest in yourself; your biggest income-generating asset is your brain.

Akwal S. Johal

'Watch your thoughts, they become your words;
watch your words, they become your actions;
watch your actions, they become your habits;
watch your habits, they become your character;
watch your character, it becomes your destiny.'
- Lao Tzu

I n her book, 'The Absorbent Mind,' Maria Montessori describes how a child's early years are incredibly important as they shape the person they become.[2] A child's brain is like a sponge; it soaks up huge amounts of information from the child's environment. Children absorb everything around them effortlessly, continuously, and indiscriminately through their senses. This is important because many of our habits are formed during childhood.

Cashflow pattern for the Learner stage

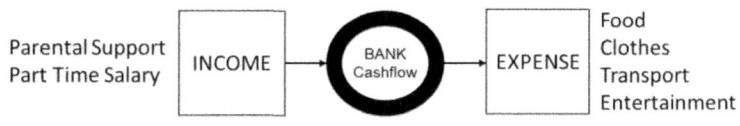

Stage 1: The Learner is categorised as Asset Poor-Time Rich.

This diagram shows the cashflow pattern for a typical 18-year-old student living at home and working part-time. Their income would be parental support and a small salary from their part-time job. Their expenses are mostly essentials like food, clothing, transport, and entertainment.

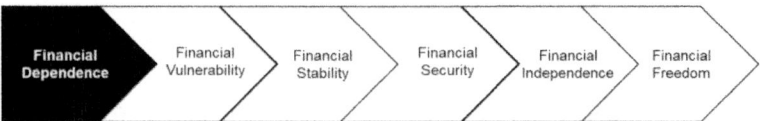

The *Financial Dependence* milestone describes a situation where you are financially dependent on your parents for essentials like food, clothing and a roof over your head. This is why the KPIs are N/A for this milestone.

Playing games is often a good way for children to learn as it's fun. I learned how to handle money at an early stage by counting the coins in my Mum's purse and playing Monopoly all day during the summer holidays. I loved being the banker, buying properties, and seeing the cash pile up. The other game I loved playing when I was growing up was Chess because it helps you to plan forward and think strategically. The best Chess players can think of many moves ahead.

I also learned a lot about mental strength, remaining positive, handling pressure, and never giving up from sports such as golf. Golf taught me to believe in myself. I knew I had a good swing, but the only thing stopping me from scoring well was me. I was getting in the way of myself. I did not have mental strength. To play to your potential, you need to believe in yourself. Golf taught me to persevere, trust myself, and focus on my goal.

Some of the most useful things I learned were not from textbooks but from my environment. A good work ethic, living within your means, and putting some money aside as savings are all habits I learned from a very young age from my parents.

Good work ethic

Dad wanted to raise his children as honest, hard-working, independent citizens.

Growing up, he would tell us stories from the lives of our Gurus. One of his favourite stories would be about Guru Nanak. While on his spiritual journey, the Guru was invited by a wealthy man to eat at his home, where he had laid on a feast fit for a king. However, the Guru chose to eat bread at a poor villager's home instead. When the wealthy man heard, he asked the Guru why he did not come to his house to eat. The Guru picked up the poor villager's bread in one hand and the rich man's cake in the other and squeezed. Milk poured from the bread, and blood poured from the cake, signifying that the poor man had earned his money through honest means and the rich man through being dishonest and exploiting the poor. The rich man realised the error of his ways and became a follower of the Guru. These childhood stories may seem trivial, but they become ingrained into a child's mind and will hopefully help them make the right choices as an adult.

A strong work ethic developed from observing how hard both my parents worked. Growing up, Dad worked nights in a bakery, and Mum worked in a laundry whilst raising three children. My first job was the paper round, delivering newspapers to people's houses for the local corner shop before going to school each morning. I was twelve years old. I enjoyed having my own money, which I could spend on whatever I wanted, mostly comics at the time. My parents did not try to control what I spent my money on. As far as they were concerned, it was my money, and I needed to learn the value of hard work and how to manage my own money. These actions became habits. It was quite common for me to take on part-time jobs during the weekends and school holidays while growing up.

Dad was fiercely independent; he believed we should stand on our own two feet, never beg or rely on charity, and most importantly, never be a burden to others. He never compared himself to other people or copied them. He set his own benchmark. I wanted to be like my Dad, hard-working and fiercely independent.

Living within your means

Mum's golden rule was to live within your means and never borrow. Her passion was Bollywood movies. She used to love taking us to the cinema to watch the latest blockbuster movie when we were young. When the cinemas shut down, with the advent of the Video Cassette Recorder (VCR) and video piracy in the 1980s, she had nowhere to go to watch her favourite Indian films. We had only just about got a colour television, and Dad was not going to waste his money on a VCR.

She worked full-time in the hospital laundry department and saved her money. Eventually, Mum bought a state-of-the-art Panasonic VCR, which included a remote control with her savings for £750, which was a lot of money back then.

Mum showed us how to live within our means and to never borrow. She got everything she ever wanted in her life without ever being in debt. I wanted to be emotionally intelligent and financially smart like my Mum.

As we did not have a lot of money growing up, I was naturally careful with money and hated seeing waste. I view this as a positive trait. Poverty was my teacher. Coming from nothing, you made every penny count.

My parents never asked what I did with the money I earned from my part-time jobs. However, I do remember buying a brand-new Monopoly board game from Woolworths. When I got home, I was quizzed as to how much it cost, and I remember lying to Mum, saying that it only cost £5 when the real price was £9! Mum thought that £5 was too much. I felt so guilty the next day that I returned it, got my money back, and carried on playing with the old set.

We all know someone who makes ends meet using their credit cards. They always seem to have the latest mobile phones, designer clothes, trainers, etc. What they fail to recognise is that the reason they have credit card debts is they spend more than they earn. It is that simple!

Many years ago, I tried to help a good friend who was struggling with their finances. I went through their bank statements and was shocked to see how much they were spending as a family on mobile phones. When I asked them about their mobile phone bill, they refused to cut back to a cheaper phone or tariff. They justified this on the basis that all the other kids at school had the same phones. Unsurprisingly, they are still in the same financial situation today as they were back then.

Growing up, if we could not afford something, we would simply do without it. We did not have a lot of money, but what we had was paid for in full. We would save up and buy that item with our own money rather than borrow and make ourselves poorer and the banks rich!

Putting some money aside as savings

Dad helped me open my first savings account at the age of nine. I remember him taking me down to the Post Office to open a savings book. It is important for children to get a physical book, as they get to keep it, take it home and see their money grow. I enjoyed watching my money grow and earn interest. I got a real buzz out of watching my savings get bigger every time I updated my book.

These early behaviours become habits which become a part of your character. My parents understood the importance of developing good behaviour from a young age.

During the learner stage, the best way for a young adult to develop is through education, becoming self-aware, surrounding themselves with positive people, and seeking a mentor.

Education

The best way to increase your income potential is to invest in yourself. Your biggest income-generating asset is your brain. A good education is one of the best investments you can make. You must believe in yourself and back yourself.

Education opens doors and can increase your ability to earn more income, but on its own does not guarantee wealth. Building wealth has more to do with your behaviour than your ability to generate more income from a good education. There are plenty of highly educated people, such as teachers, doctors, engineers, scientists, and so on, who retire penniless due to financial illiteracy.

As their incomes rise, so do their expenses. They begin to buy liabilities, believing they are buying assets. They fall into the trap of trying to keep up with the Joneses, so they buy larger properties, luxury cars, holiday homes abroad, and so on. These liabilities make them poorer as they take money out of their bank account. And if the purchase is funded by debt, this becomes a double whammy, as they have to pay back the capital plus interest. Borrowing is the equivalent of using future income to pay for today's lifestyle, and this is why some highly educated people with good incomes end up living paycheck to paycheck and retire with very little.

Formal education opened doors and provided me with a well-paid and challenging career path. However, on its own, education did not offer me the financial security or independence I wanted.

Self-awareness

During this stage, young adults are learning about themselves. Understanding their true self, what does or doesn't make them tick, their strengths and weaknesses, and what they need and want.

Self-awareness will make you feel more confident and help you make better decisions as you begin to understand yourself better. Learning about yourself is important as it can help you find a more fulfilling career path that is connected to your true self.

There are huge benefits to this soft skill in the workplace. This type of emotional intelligence is a key skill, especially if you are a people person and enjoy teamwork. Some of the key benefits of self-awareness at work are:

Time Management: Being aware of your peak performance times is important for managing time. If you are most alert and energetic in the mornings, then schedule work that requires your full attention early in the day and leave the more administrative tasks to later in the afternoon.

Managing Stress: By recognising the onset of anxiety, you can change your behaviour to take more breaks and prevent burnout.

Managing People: By understanding yourself better, you can develop skills to help you understand your staff and recognise how best to influence your boss.

Career Progression: Recognising your strengths and weaknesses allows you to play to your strengths and address your weaknesses so that your work performance improves.

If you have found a career path you are passionate about, you are more likely to be successful. A career you are passionate about never feels like a hard slog because it comes naturally to you. Time flies when you enjoy yourself. The opposite is also true. If you are stuck in a dead-end job you don't enjoy, then time drags on, and work seems like an endless chore.

My son graduated from university with a degree in psychology and maths, but at the time, he did not know which career path to follow. After two years of working in the financial services industry, he realised he did not want a desk job dealing with numbers. He was a people person and a good communicator. He decided to take some time out to follow his childhood dream and travel to Australia. During this time, he had the opportunity to work, travel, reflect, and become more self-aware. When he returned, he was clear he wanted a career in sales as a recruitment consultant. He took time to understand himself better and found a career path that suited his personality, which he excels at and enjoys.

The path is the goal. A large part of our life is spent working so it is important to pick a path that you are passionate about.

Nowadays, we have a huge choice of career options available to us, yet so many young people do not know which career path they want to pursue. Only the lucky few know, from a young age, what they want to do. Most young people go on to university to study a course they do not pursue as a career. Many leave university, move from job to job, and 'fall into' a job that becomes their career, and before long, they wonder how they got there.

Search internally, and look out for the little clues. Sometimes, they stare at you in the face and yet are invisible. Ask yourself what brings you joy. What sparks your interest? And what turns you off?

A close friend of mine seemed lost for many years, looking for her true vocation in life. She tried many different jobs, and one day, the penny dropped, and realised she was always good with animals. All her life, she was surrounded by dogs growing up and was a huge dog lover. Today, she has a great job as a dog hydro-therapist and a neat little business offering dog massage therapy.

Environment

*'You are the average of the five people you
spend the most time with.' - Jim Rohn*

Growing up, a key part of your environment is the friends you spend the most amount of time with. A huge influence on your outlook on life, your beliefs and habits come from the people around you.

You need to surround yourself with people who are aspirational, positive, and heading in the same direction as you. Hanging around with the wrong crowd can lead you in a very different direction and have a profoundly negative influence on your life.

Often, this means making difficult decisions. It may mean dropping certain people from your life. The reason I got into so much trouble with the police when I was a teenager was the friends I kept; this reminds me of another story.

A scorpion was sitting by the banks of a river and was wondering how to get across. It sees a passing frog and asks it to carry him on its back across the water. The frog hesitates and says, 'But you will sting me!' The scorpion replies, 'I would not do that because if I sting you, we will both drown.' The frog agrees to carry the scorpion across, and halfway across the river, the scorpion stings the frog. 'Why did you sting me?' asks the frog. 'I couldn't help it,' replied the scorpion. 'It's what I do.'

The moral of the story is:

Choose your friends carefully and keep a small circle. You don't need many friends, just a few good ones.

Be wary of people who befriend you and take advantage of your generosity.

Be careful who you surround yourself with. Spend time with people who bring out the best in you and are headed in the same direction.

If someone shows you who they are, believe them.

Mentor

A mentor is an experienced and trusted person who gives educational and career advice.

This is an often underutilised method of learning. Having an experienced and relevant mentor can be an invaluable privilege as they are there to listen and advise you during a critical time in your life when you need guidance due to your lack of experience and knowledge.

I was privileged enough to have a mentor allocated to me at school. My parents were not able to advise me as their exposure was limited. However, my headmaster picked me out and found a mentor for me. I had told my headmaster I wanted to become an accountant; however, I had no idea what it involved or what steps I needed to take.

I was put in touch with a partner at an accountancy firm in London who talked to me about my career choice, what type of university degree courses to select, and how to apply for jobs in the future. This was invaluable and timely for me, as I could easily have made the wrong decision.

The key to mentorship is finding someone who is approachable, listens to you, understands what you want, and, above all, is experienced and successful in the subject matter.

Be careful who you take advice from. There are many experts out there, most of whom have not been there themselves. *They are secondary experts, not primary experts.* They have studied the subject and have a sound theoretical understanding, as opposed to having a *lived experience.* This reminds me of the story about the management consultant.

A senior management consultant from one of the prestigious consultancy firms was on holiday with his family in the Caribbean. After settling into the hotel, they headed out to the beach to get some well-earned rest and relaxation.

After an hour or so, the consultant gets a bit restless and decides to go for a walk along this beautiful beach. He comes across a man lying down on the beach relaxing, smoking his cigar, and enjoying a glass of rum. Above the man was a sign saying, 'Boats for Hire.'

The consultant strikes up a conversation and asks him, 'Do you have a boat for me to hire?' To which the man replied, 'No sir, all the boats are out today.'

Intrigued by his response, the consultant quizzes the man. 'How many boats do you have?' to which the man replies, 'I have three boats, sir.'

This got the consultant thinking, and he began advising the man to take out a business loan and buy a fleet of boats to hire out. After a few years, he could expand the business to the other islands and buy a fleet of bigger boats, hire some staff, and offer excursions and experiences to tourists. After a few years, sell the business through an initial public offering (IPO) and make a huge amount of money. And by the way, I can help you with your business plan, arrange finance, and assist with selling your business.

The man looked up at the consultant and asked, 'Thank you, that all sounds marvellous, but what will I do after that?' to which the consultant replied, 'You could relax, lie down on the beach all day, smoke your favourite cigar and enjoy a glass of rum!'

The moral of the story is:

> If you want to take advice, speak to someone who has first-hand experience in the field and has been there themselves.

> The advisor needs to understand what you want, not what they think you want.

> Beware of people offering advice with vested interests.

Next, we'll look at how to break the cycle of living paycheck to paycheck.

NOTES

CHAPTER 2.2:
The Rat Race

An endless, self-defeating, pointless pursuit.

The more you make, the more you spend;
the more you spend, the more you borrow.
The more you borrow, the more you have to work;
the more you have to work, the more you make...

_____

S tage 2: The Rat Race is categorised as Asset Poor-Time Poor. Typically, you will have completed your formal education and are now working or running your own business.

You wake up, go to work, pay the bills and go to bed ... the next day, you wake up, and the cycle continues. This is the rat race, an endless, self-defeating, pointless pursuit. Whatever money comes in goes out again, and by the end of the month, you have nothing to show for all your hard work. You feel like you are working hard only to make your employer, the government, the banks and the landlord rich!

This is potentially one of the longest stages, ranging from 20 to 65 years old. Most people stay in the rat race until they retire in their mid-60s unless they have a plan B, a backup plan.

During the rat race stage, you move from *Financial Vulnerability* to *Financial Stability*. This can be achieved by increasing your income, and perhaps more significantly for most people, by changing your behaviour.

By looking at the cashflow pattern for the Rat Race Stage, we will see that many low and middle-income families live paycheck to paycheck and are *Financially Vulnerable.*

Cashflow pattern for a low-income family

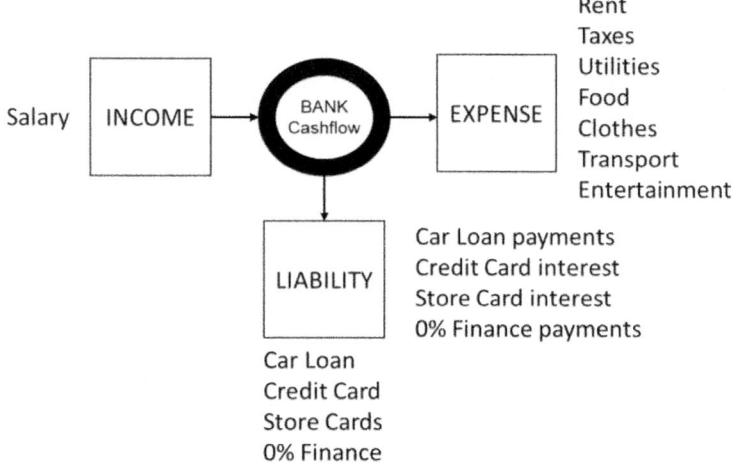

This diagram shows the cashflow pattern for a typical low-income family living in rented accommodation. Their income would be close to minimum wage. A large part of their income would go on rent, and once they have paid for their normal living costs, they have very little left.

We can see from the diagram that low-income families make their money principally by trading their time for money along the horizontal axis, the Income Statement, and supplement this with short-term debt.

Many low-income families live paycheck to paycheck; whatever comes in goes out again.

Cashflow pattern for a middle-income family

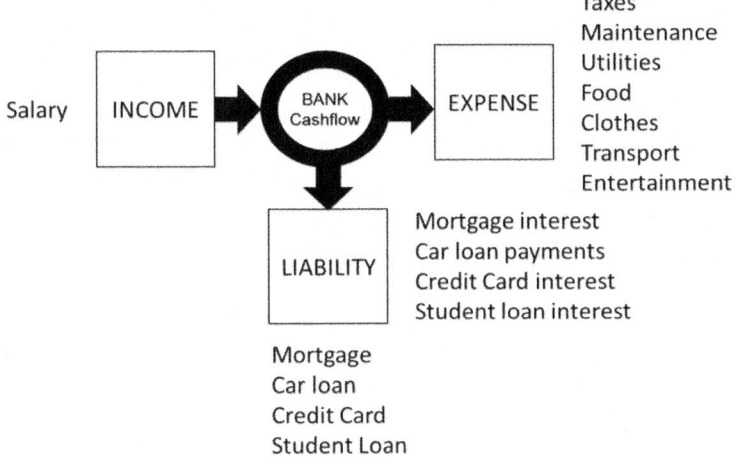

This diagram shows the cashflow pattern for a typical middle-income family who own their home. They earn a good income, but a large part of it goes on mortgage payments, and once they have paid for their normal day-to-day living costs, they have very little left.

From the cashflow pattern, we can see that middle-income families also make their money principally by trading their time for money along the horizontal line, the Income Statement, but as their incomes rise so do their expenses and they begin to accumulate liabilities.

Many middle-income families also live paycheck to paycheck; whatever comes in goes out again.

As your income rises, so does your expenditure. Middle-income families take out a larger mortgage to buy a bigger home and a larger car loan to buy a more prestigious car. Middle-income families make the classic mistake of thinking they are buying assets, but in fact, they are buying liabilities because, by definition, your home and car take money out of your pocket.

The concept that the more you make, the more you spend is called lifestyle inflation. Your spending goes up in line with your income to fund a more comfortable lifestyle, which you then become accustomed to, and in turn, you must keep working to pay off the mortgage, car loan, and credit card payments. The more debt you have, the more likely you are to remain dependent on your employer and trapped in the rat race.

Many low and middle-income families live paycheck to paycheck, with very little savings kept as an emergency buffer. This is a state called financial vulnerability. Many low and middle-income families live on a knife edge and are just one or two paychecks away from going broke.

This is borne out by research conducted by the Resolution Foundation, which found that approximately one-third of adults have little or no savings, leaving them financially vulnerable and ill-equipped to respond to unexpected bills or loss of income.[3]

The KPIs for the Financial Vulnerability milestone are:

Cashflow: You don't have a positive cashflow, or
Savings Cover: You have < 3 mths of expenses set aside as savings, or
Short-Term Debt: You haven't cleared your short-term debt, such as payday loans, credit cards, overdrafts, store cards, car loans, personal loans, 0% finance, etc.
Debt Free: You do not live debt-free.
Passive Income > Expenses: Your passive income is < expenses.

You are financially vulnerable if you do not satisfy **all** the first three KPIs: positive cashflow, savings cover and short-term debt.

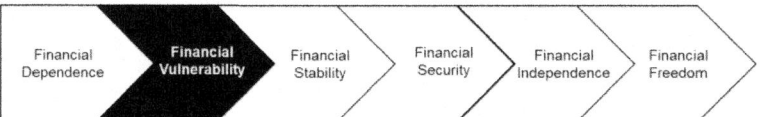

During the rat race phase, we want to move from *Financial Vulnerability* to *Financial Stability*. This can be achieved in two ways: by increasing your income and changing your behaviour.

INCREASE YOUR INCOME

The best way to increase your earned income is to invest in yourself. Your single biggest income-generating asset is your brain. Upskilling is a good way to improve your marketability; the more skills you have, the more opportunities open up.

You can earn more income by taking on extra hours, getting a second job, or working towards that promotion; however, this has its limits and is not always in your control or guaranteed.

My preference is a side hustle. The term 'side hustle' means you develop a business in parallel to your main job. You have earned income from your day job and simultaneously earn a secondary income stream.

There is a huge choice of digital services and physical side hustles available to create a second source of income alongside your day job. Using your passions, hobbies, and skills, you can start up a side hustle from home. For example, online tutoring, becoming an influencer, starting your own podcast, creating a YouTube channel, creating online courses, becoming a delivery driver, selling items you make on eBay, teaching a language or a musical instrument, dance lessons, personal training, dog-walking, etc. You are only limited by your imagination.

The characteristics of a good side hustle are low barriers to entry, so it's easy and cheap to start; flexibility, so it can fit around your lifestyle; and scalability, so you can grow the business. Side hustles can be a good way to explore alternative career paths and help build new skills. There is a chance that one of these might take off, and you could earn more money from the side hustle than your day job!

While working, I invested time and money in several side hustles. Some I made money on, others I made losses, and one or two never got off the ground. That's the nature of business, but you only need one good idea to take off.

'I never lose. I either win or learn.' – Nelson Mandela

Failure and learning are part of the journey; you never really lose. You either win or learn. Even if it does not work out as you planned, you will have learned something from the process, and this will put you in a stronger position for the next time.

In my experience, people like to tell you they have made money, but they rarely talk about the losses and mistakes they made along the way. In reality, even the most successful people make mistakes and lose money; they don't talk about it until they have succeeded!

The most important attribute is to believe in yourself and never give up. If you fall at the first hurdle, dust yourself down and carry on.

Where there's a will, there's a way; where there is no will, there is no way!

After feeling burned out in my forties, I decided to take a 6-month sabbatical and explore setting up a new business venture. We looked at opening a Montessori Nursery School, and my wife and I spent a considerable amount of time in the planning and set-up phase. We applied to the local authority for permission to set up a nursery school, but unfortunately, this was declined. However, it was one of those business ventures where I did not spend too much money upfront. Most of the upfront investment was time.

I made and lost money on stocks and shares, day trading, and commodities. In the final analysis, none of these seemed to offer quality earnings that were reliable and sustainable with relatively little effort.

In the end, it was my passion for property that paid the highest dividend. I knew deep down that this side hustle would one day pay me more than my day job and that this would be my path to financial freedom as it offered reliable and sustainable income, if set up right, with relatively little effort.

If you fail your driving test on the first attempt, you don't just give up and stop driving, you re-take until you pass. Indeed, they say the best drivers are the ones who pass on their second attempt!

Don't let the fear of losing money hold you back. You will lose money. This is part of the process. Instead of giving up, with experience, learn to manage your risk. Start small; that way, you limit the amount you might lose and as you gain experience and confidence, invest more, one step at a time.

CHANGE YOUR BEHAVIOUR

For most people, building wealth has more to do with your behaviour than your ability to generate higher earned income.

Many hard-working people earn a good income but have nothing to show for it. The root cause is poor management of their cashflow. Earning money and keeping hold of money require two very different skills. Whilst education and working hard will increase your ability to earn more money, it is your behaviour, in particular spending carefully and saving for the future, which has the biggest impact on building wealth. These behaviours are best learned at a young age.

It is perfectly possible for low-income earners to become wealthy. They understand what it is like to live on very little and, therefore, can develop the drive and determination to build a better life for themselves. Poverty teaches you how to be resourceful and make every penny count. Learning how to spend your money carefully, saving a higher proportion of your income, and investing wisely will build wealth.

For those who are not convinced, consider the true story of the American janitor Ronald Read, who amassed a fortune of $8m!

You are probably asking yourself, 'How did he do that on a janitor's salary?' The fact is that you do not need to earn a huge salary to become wealthy. The secret to his wealth was maintaining a frugal lifestyle. He was economical with his spending and set aside a large portion of his take-home pay as savings. Any surplus money he had was invested in assets, and so his wealth continued to grow.

Ronald Read drove an inexpensive car. He did not eat in fancy restaurants or go on holidays. The lesson here is that behaviour is important; what you do with the money you make counts.

***Anyone can become wealthy; for most people, it has
less to do with your income level and more to
do with your behaviour.***

Ronald Read's story is an example of extreme frugality; it is not something I could do, as you need to enjoy life, too. My Mum always said it is important to work for that golden egg but have a few chocolate eggs along the way!

There is a saying: making money is action and keeping money is behaviour. The skills required to make and keep money are very different. Making money requires taking risks, believing in yourself, and putting your money where your mouth is, as opportunity waits for no one. Keeping money, on the other hand, requires being risk averse, knowing what you have can easily disappear, thinking long-term, and being content with what you have. It is keeping the money you make, rather than how much you make, that has the biggest impact on building wealth.

It's difficult to get an accurate number for lottery winners who have gone bust within a few years of winning. Estimates vary considerably from 33% to 70%. The main reason cited is the inability of lottery winners to manage the money they have won. Their lives move from ordinary to extraordinary in the blink of an eye, and they are ill-equipped to deal with it.

One of the most famous lottery winners who went bust was Jack Whittaker, who in 2002 won $314 million at the Powerball Jackpot, the biggest lottery prize in history at the time. Now, you may wonder how someone with $314 million could end up broke. When Jack was interviewed, the construction worker from West Virginia said he managed to squander his fortune by giving away most of his money to friends, family, strangers, diner waitresses, and strippers.

Research shows the main reasons lottery winners go broke within a few years of winning are giving money away to hangers-on, poorly thought-out investments, overestimating how much they thought they had won, and reckless spending.

This teaches us the importance of keeping hold of the money you have earned, which requires a completely different skill set to making money.

The secret to escaping the rat race is to break the link to debt. The following, *'Six Steps to Saving'* are a guide to keeping the money you have earned and can help get you from financial vulnerability, living paycheck to paycheck, to financial stability, one of the milestones to financial freedom.

1. Collect Data

Start by opening two bank accounts, a current and a savings account. The current account is where your salary is paid and is used for day-to-day transactions. Make sure the current account pays interest on credit balances and does not charge monthly fees. The savings account is kept to build up an emergency buffer for unexpected expenses or loss of income. This account will pay you a higher rate of interest on your balance.

If you don't have data, you can't measure; and if you can't measure, how do you know if you are improving or not?

To reduce spending, you must distinguish between a need and a want. A need is a survival necessity (rent, travel to work, food, clothing, utility bills, etc), whereas a want is a desire (a prestigious car, an expensive holiday, a flashy watch, etc). Simply put, needs are necessities, and wants are 'nice to haves.'

Next, start collecting data. Go through your monthly current account statement and categorise everything into needs and wants.

2. Eliminate any waste

The next thing to do is go through all your monthly direct debits and standing orders and review your subscriptions. Are there any regular payments going out for services that are never or rarely used, such as gym membership, magazine subscriptions, online movies, or sports channel streaming services?

If so, then cancel the subscriptions for anything you seldom or no longer use.

3. Save money on needs

Loyalty no longer pays.

Get the best deals for big-ticket items, such as utilities and insurance policies. Naively staying with one company rarely benefits you. Before you realise it, the company that offered the best deal a few years ago is now uncompetitive, and you are paying far more than you need to.

Shop around on price comparison sites for the best tariff for your gas, electric, water, phone, and broadband services.

Review your insurance policies annually for buildings, contents, boiler cover for hot water and heating, appliances, and motor vehicles. Don't just accept the annual renewal quote. Check online to see if it is still competitive, and ask your insurance company to match the best market rate if it is not. Also, if you rarely make a claim, then consider applying an excess, as this can reduce your premiums substantially.

Don't go cheap, as this can often mean paying triple! I have made the mistake of using cheap builders. This has cost me double to reverse their mistakes and triple to do the work properly the second time. More often than not, going cheap costs you triple.

4. Reduce spending on wants

Review expenditure on any unnecessary purchases and cancel where appropriate.

The term 'keeping up with the Joneses' refers to wanting to own the same possessions as your friends or neighbours simply because you are worried about falling behind socially. This is a never-ending pursuit. Once you have what everyone else has, you will meet someone new who has more than you, so the goalposts move, and the game of keeping up with the Joneses continues.

Similarly, if you are someone who always wants the latest gadget, car, or home appliance simply because 'everyone else has them,' then remember there will always be a newer version or trend just around the corner, making this year's model or trend obsolete. Again, it is a never-ending pursuit in trying to keep up with the Joneses.

This is best described by the phrase, *'the goalpost keeps moving.'* Once you have achieved your goal, you want more, as *enough is never enough.*

What is the difference between someone who has an income of £30,000 a year and spends £25,000 and someone who has an income of £100,000 a year and spends £120,000?

The lower earner will have increased their wealth by £5,000, and the higher earner will have reduced their wealth by £20,000! The lower earner has assets in the form of savings, and the high earner, who may have a more comfortable lifestyle, will have liabilities.

This simple example illustrates that, regardless of your income level, your behaviour is one of the key elements to wealth creation. I firmly believe low-income families can become wealthy as their life experience of growing up on very little and having to make every penny count gives them a huge behavioural advantage over someone who has a high income or was born into money yet is reckless with their spending.

5. Pay off your short-term debts

Mum always said, 'The best type of debt is no debt!'

Before you start putting money aside for your savings, pay off all your short-term debts as a priority. I am a great believer in living a debt-free life. However, there are a limited number of circumstances in which debt can be a good thing. Let us break debt down into two categories: good debt and bad debt.

The following are considered good debt:

Student Loans

Student Loans are generally a good idea because they are for education. Investing in yourself is usually a good idea. The benefit of a student loan is that you do not start paying it off until you start working, and your income needs to be above a certain threshold.

Mortgage

A mortgage is necessary to help you buy a home. Unless you are fortunate enough to be a cash buyer, most people will need a mortgage to buy their home.

Loans paid off by someone else

An example of this would be a Buy-to-Let mortgage on a rental property. This type of debt is good debt because someone else, the tenant, is paying off the debt for you.

The following are considered bad debt:

Payday Loans

Payday loans are short-term, extremely high-interest loans that take advantage of consumers' need for immediate credit. They are usually based on how much you earn and typically need to be paid back in 30 days.

Credit Cards

Credit cards can be a bit like your best friend or your worst enemy. You should only use them if you can pay off the full amount before the monthly due date, so there is no interest charge. If you are disciplined enough to do this every month, you can take advantage of the cashflow benefit, rewards programmes, cashback, and purchase protection benefits offered by the card companies.

Credit cards can also be your worst enemy if you find yourself unable to pay them off in full every month. You will be charged a penal interest rate if you don't clear the balance each month.

Also, if having a credit card makes you spend more due to the ease of use, it is no longer your best friend.

If any of these happen, cut it up and put it in the bin!

I found that initially, I was disciplined enough to pay off the balance each month. However, gradually, over time, I began using my credit card for everything and spending more and more due to its convenience. Using a credit card did not feel like I was parting with money as it was a digital transaction. However, after cutting up my credit cards, I started using my debit card and cash again. It felt like I was parting with money, and this helped me control my spending.

When I cut up my credit cards, I felt I was taking back control, and I have never used one since. If you can't bring yourself to cut up your card, then leave it at home; that way, you are not tempted to use it.

Store Cards

A store card is a credit card you can only use with one high street chain or group. I avoid these as they operate in much the same way as credit cards, and I like to keep my life simple and keep my cards to an absolute minimum.

0% finance or Buy Now Pay Later

These deals allow customers to buy expensive items, such as household appliances, furniture or electrical items, on zero per cent finance and spread the payments over an extended period. The main benefit is that customers do not pay interest. This means you can spread the cost over time without paying any extra.

The issue with this form of finance is that the lender, who is working with the retailer, has factored in a certain number of defaults. When you default on this type of finance, it will result in an outstanding balance, which may attract a penal rate of interest being charged.

It is best to avoid this type of deal unless you have the money set aside and want to take advantage of the cashflow benefit and pay it off in full on the due date.

Car Loans

Buying a car, which is a depreciating liability funded by a car loan on which you are paying interest, is one of the biggest mistakes I see young people make.

Everyone knows that a new car depreciates or loses about 20% of its value as soon as you drive the car off the dealer's forecourt as it is now technically second-hand.

According to the AA, the average new car will have lost 60% of its value after three years.[4] Depreciation slows as the car gets older, so you may find that a nearly new car, perhaps two or three years old, is of better value than a brand-new one.

I prefer to buy cars with my savings. It does not make sense to pay loan interest on a depreciating liability. This is a triple whammy as you are taking on debt and paying the finance company interest on the car loan, and the car is depreciating year after year. This is one of the fastest ways to destroy wealth and become poorer.

This is a classic example of people thinking they are buying an asset, but in fact, the car is a liability. A car takes money out of your bank account in the form of fuel, insurance, taxes, repairs, maintenance, roadworthiness tests and servicing.

Overdraft

An overdraft arises when you spend or withdraw more money than you have in your current account. The bank provides an overdraft facility to allow the transaction to go through, and it will typically charge interest and a fee.

An agreed overdraft limit with the bank will charge less interest and fees than one that has not been agreed.

Having to rely on an overdraft facility constantly is usually a sign of poor cashflow management.

Personal Loans

Personal loans are loans for large purchases or home improvements.

This may be a sign of living beyond your means or insufficient savings.

I am not averse to borrowing where you can afford it, but I am averse to excessive debt and bad debt. Excessive debt is one of the main reasons people struggle financially and get poorer.

The order of priority for paying off your short-term debt is to start with the most expensive debts first and work downward from there. I suggest paying down in the following order:

1. Payday Loans
2. Credit Cards
3. Store Cards
4. Car Loans
5. Overdrafts
6. Personal Loans
7. 0% Finance

6. Start building up your savings by setting aside a minimum of 10% of your take-home pay.

'Compound interest is the eighth wonder of the world. He who understands it, earns it ... he who doesn't ... pays it.'
- Albert Einstein

Why do we need to save? According to the economist Sir John Maynard Keynes, there are three reasons:

Transactional: Individuals hold money for day-to-day transactions.

Precautionary: Individuals hold money as an emergency buffer for unforeseen expenses or loss of income.

Speculative: Once you have set aside enough money for day-to-day transactions and emergencies, you can now focus on saving for speculative purposes.

Financially savvy people understand the concept of *compounding.* Simply put, it is 'interest on interest.' With savings, you not only earn interest on the capital, but you also earn interest on the interest, and this accumulates exponentially over time.

By way of example, if you deposit £100 in a savings account that pays 10% annual interest, you will have earned £10 in interest by the end of year 1, leaving a balance of £110 in the account. In Year 2, with compound interest, you will earn 10% annual interest on £110 (the £100 initial principal plus £10 interest earned in Year 1), which is £11 in interest, leaving a total balance of £121 after two years. Therefore, you can see that your savings grow at a faster rate the longer you leave your money invested. In year one, you earn £10 interest, and in year two, you earn £11. This is because you are earning interest on interest, which grows exponentially over the years.

I learned about the power of compounding when I was quite young. Dad opened a savings book for me at the local post office when I was nine years old. I would put some money aside from my pocket money, paper rounds, and summer jobs, which would pay me interest. As a child, I used to love lining up at the post office to get my savings book updated and see how quickly my money was growing.

To demonstrate the power of compounding, let us take a more dramatic example to make the point. If you had the choice between £1,000,000 today or investing a 1p coin that doubles every day for the next 30 days, which would you take?

Most people I ask would take the £1,000,000 today. But if you take out your calculator and double 1p for 30 days, you will be amazed at what you get. On day one, you start with 1p. On day two, you get 2p, and on day three, you get 4p and so on. By the end of the month, your 1p will have accumulated to an incredible £5,368,709.12!

89

Here is the proof:

Day 1	£0.01	Day 11	£10.24	Day 21	£10,485.76
Day 2	£0.02	Day 12	£20.48	Day 22	£20,971.52
Day 3	£0.04	Day 13	£40.96	Day 23	£41,943.04
Day 4	£0.08	Day 14	£81.92	Day 24	£83,886.08
Day 5	£0.16	Day 15	£163.84	Day 25	£167,772.16
Day 6	£0.32	Day 16	£327.68	Day 26	£335,544.32
Day 7	£0.64	Day 17	£655.36	Day 27	£671,088.64
Day 8	£1.28	Day 18	£1,310.72	Day 28	£1,342,177.28
Day 9	£2.56	Day 19	£2,621.44	Day 29	£2,684,354.56
Day 10	£5.12	Day 20	£5,242.88	Day 30	£5,368,709.12

You will notice that the real magic happens towards the end. If you saved for 20 days, your 1p would only be worth £5,242.88, but if you saved for an additional 10 days, your 1p would be worth an incredible £5,368,709.12. This is the power of compounding. It has a huge impact on the outcome in later years.

The reverse is also true; if you are unable to keep up with your monthly loan payments, the interest charged is capitalised and added to your balance, which grows exponentially over time as interest is charged on interest.

Banks understand the power of compounding, which is why lending is so profitable. We, too, can learn from this and act as bankers by lending our money to the banks in the form of savings.

Trying to make as much money as quickly as possible is a poor investment strategy. A high-risk/return strategy may work well once or twice, but it is neither reliable nor sustainable for the long term and, therefore, does not benefit from compounding.

On the other hand, a good investment strategy is making reasonable and repeatable returns over a long period. This is where you see the magic of compounding really work.

The key lesson is that if you are saving for your future, then you must start early. If you keep putting off saving until later, then you will be missing out on a huge opportunity to make money. The earlier you start, the better.

Mum's golden rule was to live within your means and never borrow to pay for anything other than for your home.

If you can live within your means, you will be able to save and earn compound interest. Conversely, if you live beyond your means, you will accumulate debt and pay the banks compound interest. The good news is that everyone can do this. Over time, with the power of compounding, you will become wealthier.

Mum taught me a simple budgeting rule: the first thing you do each month is to set aside 1/3rd of your salary towards your savings and then spend 1/3rd on needs and the final 1/3rd on wants.

Mum's 1/3rd budget rule ... 1/3 Saving, 1/3 Needs & 1/3 Wants.

Mum's 1/3rd budget is simple to understand and implement. As a rule of thumb, you pay yourself first, and then the balance is split equally between your needs and wants.

In the example below, the monthly budget is to set aside 1/3rd or £1,000 of your £3,000 take-home pay towards your savings, first and foremost, and then live off the remainder, allocating

1/3rd towards your needs and the remaining 1/3rd towards your wants.

Date	Description	Incoming £	Outgoing £	Save £	Needs £	Wants £
01/01/XX	Salary	3,000				
01/01/XX	Transfer to Savings Account		(1,000)	(1,000)		
03/01/XX	Drinks with friends		(200)			(200)
07/01/XX	Travel		(100)		(100)	
08/01/XX	Groceries		(120)		(120)	
11/01/XX	Rent including utilities		(750)		(750)	
15/01/XX	Entertainment		(100)			(100)
15/01/XX	Restaurant		(200)			(200)
19/01/XX	Holiday		(400)			(400)
20/01/XX	Clothing		(30)		(30)	
26/01/XX	Subscriptions - Gym, TV		(100)			(100)
	Total	**3,000**	**(3,000)**	**(1,000)**	**(1,000)**	**(1,000)**
	Target			33%	33%	33%

If you live at home saving 1/3rd is achievable, if not, then there are no hard and fast rules about how much to set aside as savings each month, as it depends on your personal circumstances and how quickly you want to achieve financial independence. *Nevertheless, as a minimum you should set aside at least 10% of your take-home pay, and split the balance between your needs and wants, according to your personal circumstances.* The important point is, you are building up your savings, and the more you can save the quicker you will reach your goals.

Initially, build up your savings to 1 month of your normal expenditure, which provides coverage for any one-off emergencies. That way, you do not go overdrawn or into debt if there is an unexpected expense, such as a parking fine, a or delay in receiving your income. In this example, if your normal monthly expenditure is £2,000, then initially try to build up an emergency buffer of £2,000.

Once that is achieved, the next step should be to build up your savings to 3 months of your normal expenditure. That way, if you lose your job, you can cover three months' worth of expenses, which is enough time to find a new job, avoiding the need to go overdrawn or into debt. Therefore, if your normal monthly expenditure is £2,000, build up an emergency buffer of £6,000.

If successful, you will have transitioned from *Financial Vulnerability* to *Financial Stability*. You now feel in control of your money and not the other way around. You have managed to control your spending habits, paid off your short-term debt, and set aside enough money as an emergency buffer.

Cashflow pattern for Financial Stability milestone

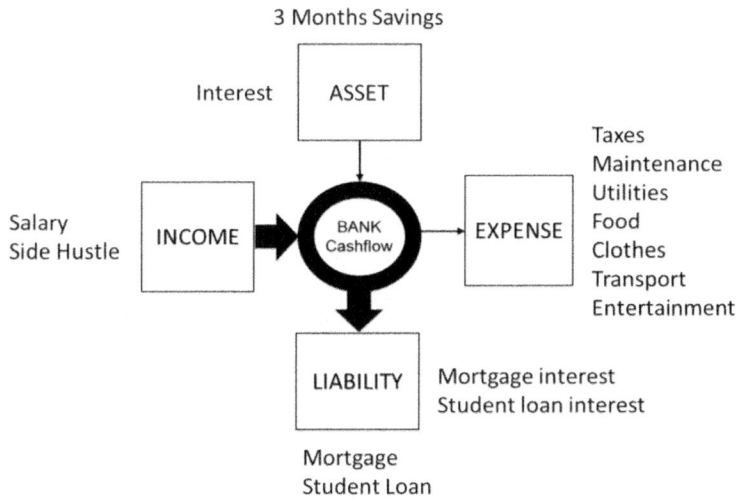

You transition to *Financial Stability* when you satisfy **all** the first three KPIs: positive cashflow, savings cover and short-term debt.

The KPIs for the Financial Stability milestone are:

Cashflow: You have a positive cashflow.
Savings Cover: You have 3+ months of expenses set aside as savings.
Short-Term Debt: You have cleared your short-term debt
Debt Free: You do not live debt-free.
Passive Income > Expenses: Your passive income < expenses.

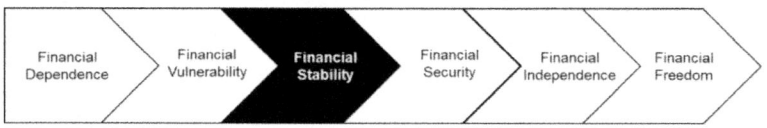

During the rat race, there is a transition in the cashflow pattern from *Financial Vulnerability* to *Financial Stability*, which can be summarised as:

Make income from your job
Pay bills
Live off what is left or borrow

to

Make income from your job and side hustles
Pay yourself first
Pay bills
Live off what is left

It is a mathematical certainty that if you spend more than you earn, you will rely on short-term debt such as credit cards.

Expense > Income = Short Term Debt

If you spend less than you earn, you will start to save.

Income > Expense = Saving

The choice for me was clear: either I saved knowing that I would reach my goal of financial freedom by the age of 50, or not save and become someone who must have to work for financial reasons into my mid-sixties.

And for those cynics that say, I do not have any money left to set aside, I say try it; don't dismiss it until you have tried it. Pay yourself first by setting aside a proportion of your salary and live off the remainder. Human nature is highly adaptive, and it is possible to adjust to a more frugal lifestyle while still living comfortably. At some point, you will start feeling good about having the money you have earned set aside, and as it grows, it will motivate you to continue. Having money set aside will make you feel less financially vulnerable and stressed. You will sleep better knowing that you have an emergency buffer to absorb any unexpected expenses or loss of income.

I bought my first luxury car in my thirties and my second in my forties, but these were paid for outright with my savings. I bought my cars 2-3 years old with low mileage; that way, I was not paying the 20% premium for the prestige of owning a new car. Of course, I could easily go out and buy a flashy new car any day, but I choose not to. Why would I want to make someone else rich? I am not here to make the car dealership or the bank any richer, no more than I am here to keep up appearances to impress others. My plan was to play the long game and achieve financial freedom.

It's not easy following your own path and being an outlier by choosing not to copy those around you. In addition to social pressures, the media bombard us daily with constant advertising. For the younger generation, this has got a whole lot worse with mobile phones and social media. We are sold on the dream that is the big house, the flashy new car, the expensive watch, the fabulous vacations, etc. We fall for this marketing ploy to part with our money as we want to keep up with our peer group and not be seen as falling behind socially.

Material possessions rarely bring respect and admiration. The solution is not found outside with more possessions but internally with being content, humble, and respectful to others.

You might think having possessions will bring you respect and admiration, but nothing could be further from reality. What it will invite is envy and a bunch of fake friends. Respect is earned, not bought. Being a good friend, being humble, and helping others will bring you respect. As for admiration, it is your accomplishments and actions that bring admiration from other people, not material possessions.

Remember, when you buy these possessions, you are not buying assets; you are buying liabilities because they take money out of your bank account, and if you fall for this, you can end up broke.

I was stuck in the rat race in my 30s, working long hours and living paycheck to paycheck. I worked primarily for big banks, and before long, I was slipping into becoming that corporate guy I never wanted to be. I had a good job, working in investment banking on a good salary, yet I was utterly miserable. When I worked for Dresdner Kleinwort Benson, I would regularly catch a cab home at 2 a.m. in the morning and be back in the office by 8 a.m. My effort-to-reward ratio was poor. I was time-poor and asset-poor and felt like I was being sucked deeper and deeper into the rat race with no way out. This job was one of the lowest points in my career.

On other days, I would have visions of an older version of me in a grey suit, carrying a briefcase, walking down the escalators in the subway. I knew I did not want to be that guy. *I was living to work, not working to live.* Deep down, I knew this was not something for me long-term; this was not my vision.

Being financially savvy and having the self-belief to follow my path enabled me to build a healthy passive income while I was working. Working for someone else became a means to an end rather than an end in itself.

The next chapter explains how it's possible to escape the rat race and become independently wealthy.

NOTES

CHAPTER 2.3:

The Investor

Good investing is not making lots of money as quickly as possible, but making reasonable and repeatable returns over a long period of time.

*Making money is action, keeping money is behaviour
and growing money is knowledge.*

S tage 3: The Investor is categorised as Asset Rich - Time Poor. Typically, you are in full-time employment, developing your side hustle, striving to live debt-free and generating a passive income stream by acquiring assets. Over time, your passive income will grow and become a greater proportion of your total income. You are growing less and less dependent on your paycheck.

During the investor stage, you are moving from:

Financial Stability to *Financial Security* by living debt-free, and from

Financial Security to *Financial Independence* by buying income-generating assets.

Let us look at each of these in detail.

LIVING DEBT FREE

'If you don't have leverage, you don't get in trouble. That's the only way a smart person can go broke. And as I have always said, "If you are smart, you don't need it; and if you are dumb, you shouldn't be using it."' - Warren Buffett

Over the lifetime of your mortgage, on average, you will be paying back double what you originally borrowed. Let's look at the cost of a typical mortgage over its lifetime. Say you borrow £200,000 at a 5% interest rate over a 25-year term.

Repayment Mortgage

With a repayment mortgage, you pay back interest and capital each month, so you will have nothing outstanding by the end of the term.

Over the lifetime of the repayment mortgage, you will be paying £150,754 in interest. This means you will pay back a total of £350,754 (£200,000 capital + £150,754 interest) over 300 months (25 years x 12 months), giving a monthly repayment of £1,169 (£350,754 / 300).[5]

With a repayment mortgage, you will be paying back a factor of 1.75x what you borrowed (£350,754/£200,000) over its lifetime!

Interest Only Mortgage

With an interest-only mortgage, you only pay back the interest each month and must separately make provision to pay back the capital at the end of the term.

Now, let's take the example of an interest-only mortgage. Under the same terms as above, over the lifetime of the mortgage, you will be paying £250,000 in interest. This figure is higher than a repayment mortgage because the original capital remains outstanding throughout and needs to be paid back in full at the end.

Your monthly repayments will be £833.33 = (£200,000 x 5%)/12. Over the lifetime of the mortgage, this is an interest cost of £250,000 (£833.33 x 300). Thus, you will pay back a total of £450,000 (£200,000 capital + £250,000 interest).[5]

With an interest-only mortgage, you will be paying back a factor of 2.25x what you borrowed (£450,000/£200,000) over its lifetime!

> *Over the lifetime of your mortgage, on average,*
> *you will be paying back double what you borrowed!*

Although mortgages are secured on property and attract a lower interest rate than unsecured debt, you should aim to fully redeem your mortgage as soon as possible after all your other debts are paid off. The best way to redeem your mortgage is to overpay each month or make regular partial capital repayments, as and when you can afford it, without incurring fees. The capital amount is reduced; therefore, you can clear the mortgage earlier and pay less interest.

Using the repayment mortgage example above, if you overpay your mortgage by £90 per month (by paying £1,259 per month), you would clear the mortgage in just 22 years, cutting the term by three years and saving £22,466 in interest![5]

> *If you aim to live debt-free,*
> *why would you need a credit score?*

Mortgage brokers and banks, of course, recommend keeping your mortgage for the full term as they would argue this is a cheap way to borrow and a way of maintaining your credit score. Moreover, they recommend topping up your mortgage to take advantage of any equity in the property. I have never understood this logic. If you aim to live debt-free, why would you need a credit score or to increase your mortgage? Mortgage brokers and banks have a vested interest in keeping you in debt. Follow your plan, and what feels right to you. You cannot put a price on financial security for your family.

I made regular partial capital repayments and watched the capital balance and monthly interest payments fall dramatically. In my early forties, I fully redeemed my mortgage within nine years. I received a copy of my title deeds and remember the feeling. It was like having a huge burden disappear. Knowing that you have the financial security of owning your property outright and that no one can ever take the roof over your head away is an important step towards reaching your goal.

Mum always said that the best type of debt is no debt! By paying off your long-term debts, such as your student loan and mortgage, you put yourself in a strong position to reach financial freedom.

> *'Never risk what we have and need*
> *for what we don't have and don't need.'*
> *- Warren Buffett*

Once you become debt-free, never take out any more debt or put your home at risk. We are constantly under pressure to keep up with our peers, buy a larger home, a luxury car, an expensive watch, go on fabulous holidays, etc. That is all great when credit is cheap, but once interest rates start rising or you lose your job, you will struggle to keep up with the payments and risk losing your home.

Once you have paid off your long-term debts, such as student loans and mortgages, you will have achieved *Financial Security*. You are now living debt-free and will feel financially secure because you and your family can no longer lose the roof over your heads.

Cashflow pattern for the Financial Security milestone

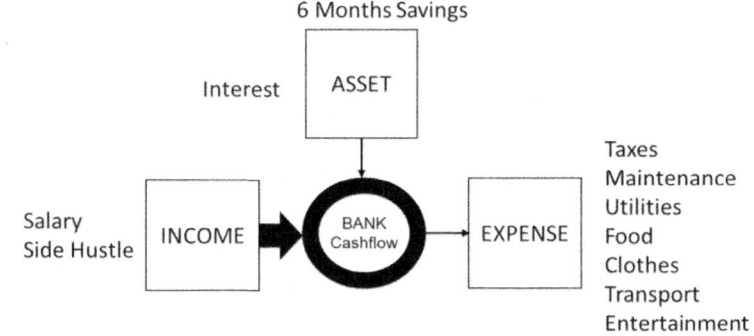

The KPIs for the Financial Security milestone are:

Cashflow: You have a positive cashflow.

Savings Cover: You have 6+ months of expenses set aside as savings.

Short-Term Debt: You have cleared your short-term debt

Debt Free: You live debt-free.

Passive Income > Expenses: Your passive income < expenses.

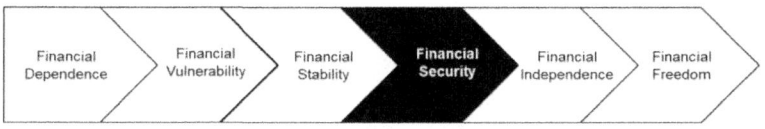

BUYING INCOME-GENERATING ASSETS

It is a myth to say that passive income requires no effort.

There are two types of income: earned and passive income. Earned income is income generated from working; you exchange your labour for money. This could be income generated from employment, running your own business or a side hustle. Passive income, on the other hand, is income generated from assets.

There is no such thing as zero-effort passive income. It is a myth to say that passive income requires no effort. You will need to conduct research, carry out investment appraisals, buy, sell and monitor performance. This takes time, but the effort-to-reward ratio can be very good.

When I look for assets to invest in, I look for quality earnings which meet the following criteria:

Reliable: The cashflow comes in regular month-on-month.

Sustainable: The cashflow will continue in the long term.

Robust: The underlying business model is strong, and there will always be demand.

Inflation proof: The cashflow will increase over time.

Effort to reward ratio: Low effort - High reward.

Let us look at some of the most common ways to generate a passive income. We covered savings earlier. Here, we will briefly cover the pros and cons of some of the more common income-generating assets, such as stock market investments, pension funds, commodity trading, peer-to-peer lending and then look at property in more detail.

If you are risk averse, savings are one of the safest ways to grow money. However, they offer a fairly low rate of return, which may not always keep up with inflation. However, if you are a risk taker, you may be attracted to riskier investments that offer the potential for higher returns.

It is fine to take a calculated risk, but do not take a blind risk in the hope of huge returns; that is gambling, not investing. It is like putting your money on the horses.

Stock Market

If you don't want to own your own business, the next best thing you could do is invest in the stock market and become the owner of a fraction of a company. The Stock Market is one of the most accessible ways to invest in a business, generating a dividend income and capital appreciation. The average rate of return in the stock market over the long term is 7-9% pa.[6]

Dividend Stocks and Shares

If you invest in the shares of a company, then you own a fraction of that company. An investor in the shares of a company is called a shareholder. As a shareholder, you are entitled to a vote, dividends and the right to sell your shares.

Companies issue shares to raise capital. Private company shares are not listed, so they are unavailable for the general public to buy and sell. However, public companies have their shares listed on the stock market, where they can be bought and sold. Shares in public companies are traded on stock exchanges such as the London Stock Exchange (LSE), New York Stock Exchange (NYSE), etc.

The main advantages of investing in the stock market are low barriers to entry, so it is easy to get started. High liquidity so you can convert your assets back into cash easily, money can be earned in two ways through dividend income and capital gains, and finally, it is easy to monitor the performance of your investment as stock prices are quoted in real-time and are public information.

The disadvantages of investing in the stock market are that you have no control over the fate of your business and your capital is at risk.

The stock market is not for everyone. Shares are traded daily, and their prices move up and down in real-time. You can easily get caught up in the moment and overreact to short-term market volatility. It is not unusual for share prices to drop 20% in one day, and you panic sell while the market is low.

Although share prices can be volatile in the short term, the stock market generally performs well over the long term. When investing, this should be for the long-term, so 5+ years, and you should ignore any short-term volatility.

Individual company shares are one type of investment and suit passive investors who adopt a 'buy and hold' strategy and play the long game. However, the disadvantage is that you have all your eggs in one basket, and if that company were to collapse, you could lose your entire investment.

If you don't want to invest in single company shares, there are several options available for passive investors, such as Mutual Funds and Index Funds.

Mutual Funds

Mutual Funds are professionally managed funds that invest in a broad range of securities such as money market deposits, fixed-rate bonds, shares, etc.

The main advantages of a mutual fund are diversification and professional management of your money. However, the main disadvantage is the management charge, which can eat into your profit.

Index Funds

Index Funds are a type of mutual fund that, as the name suggests, tracks a market index, such as the FTSE100, which tracks the 100 largest public companies on the London Stock Exchange, or the S&P500, which tracks the 500 largest public companies in the US.

The main advantages of index funds are diversification, good long-term results, and a cost-effective way to invest in the stock market, as these index funds do not require a professional fund manager.

The main disadvantage of index funds is the lack of flexibility, as you could miss out on smaller, high-growth companies.

Pension Funds

A pension fund is a retirement plan where you and/or your employer contribute to a pool of funds, and upon retirement, you receive a lump sum payment and a pension income for life.

The size of your pension fund depends on two factors. Firstly, how much has been contributed and secondly, the fund performance. By their nature, pension funds are long-term investments.

The main advantages of pension funds are that you may get tax relief on your contributions, the fund benefits from the power of compounding, and there is typically a tax-free lump sum option to take on retirement.

The main disadvantages of a pension fund are poor liquidity, as there is no access to your funds until a certain age, risk of poor returns and management charges, which can be quite substantial.

Commodities (Gold, Silver, Copper, etc)

Trading in commodities can generate capital gains.

The main advantages of gold are that it can be held as a hedge against economic downturns and it is highly liquid as it can be easily converted to cash. The main disadvantage of physical gold is the storage costs.

Peer-to-Peer (P2P) Lending

P2P lending is a way to lend to individuals and businesses by cutting out the banks as the middlemen. P2P lending websites connect borrowers directly with lenders.

The main advantages of P2P lending are higher rates of return than ordinary saving rates offered by banks, as well as low barriers to entry and diversification.

The main disadvantage is that some borrowers might not be able to pay you back. This is called default risk. Other disadvantages include low liquidity, as you may not be able to get your money back immediately in an emergency, risk of late payment, risk of the P2P site going bust, and the fees charged can eat into your profits.

Rental Property

Rental properties are the ultimate form of passive income.

Ray Kroc, the founder of McDonald's, once asked a group of MBA students to tell him what business they thought he was in. 'You are in the business of selling hamburgers, of course,' someone said. 'No,' he replied. 'My business is property.'

McDonald's owns some of the most valuable real estate around the world. Under its business model, many franchisees pay McDonald's an initial franchisee fee, royalties, and rent.

Instead of just making money from franchisee fees and royalties, McDonald's also became the landlord to its franchisees. McDonald's purchases properties and leases them to their franchisees for huge rental income. Simply put, franchisees fund the purchase of McDonald's properties!

There are many ways to make money in the property market. For instance, you could buy and hold properties for capital appreciation, develop and sell old properties, flip off-plan new build properties, become a sourcing agent for high-end buyers, become a specialist rental agent for landlords, provide maintenance services, provide inventory management services or lend short-term capital to developers to name a few.

With rental properties, the aim is to get the tenant to pay off your loan so you end up with a debt-free property that has appreciated in value. This seems very similar to McDonald's business model, where someone else pays off the loan on your property.

The pros of rental properties are:

Tangible Asset: You are investing in bricks and mortar. You have ownership of something physical and tangible. You can see it, touch it and feel it, unlike many financial assets.

Passive Income: Property is often considered the ultimate form of passive income. Rental properties produce a passive income stream that, once set up, will require very little ongoing maintenance. It is good quality earnings. By this, I mean the business model is robust, and the rental income is reliable and sustainable.

Effort-to-reward ratio: If set up correctly, the rewards relative to the effort can be very appealing.

Hedge against inflation: Rental income generally rises over time, so it acts as a natural hedge against inflation.

Slow and cyclical: Unlike the stock market, which is volatile, the property market is slow and cyclical and, therefore, easier to predict. You have more time to think, plan and evaluate opportunities.

Necessity: There will always be a demand for property as a place to live.

Appreciating Asset: In addition to generating a passive income, there is the added benefit of owning an asset which can appreciate in the long term.

Flexibility: As this is a physical asset, there is the opportunity to develop and increase market value and improve rental yield.

Tax Breaks: Property investing currently has some of the best tax breaks available, which are not available to other forms of investing. You are allowed to deduct certain expenses, such as loan interest and allowable operating costs, from your rental income when working out your taxable profit.

Pension: Rental income is an alternative to a pension fund. It has the advantage of keeping up with inflation and can be passed down upon death to your children.

The cons of rental properties are:

High Barriers to Entry: The barriers to entry in terms of time and money are high compared to other forms of investment. To invest in property, you typically require a significant deposit and access to credit. You will need to search for suitable rental properties, carry out investment appraisals, and liaise with estate agents, solicitors, surveyors, builders, and tenants.

Poor Liquidity: If you need to convert your asset into cash, you need to allow several months or longer to sell your property to get hold of the money.

Bad Tenants: If you are unfortunate enough to have a tenant that damages your property, you will need to evict the tenant and deal with all the repairs to get the property back to a rental standard. In such cases, the security deposit may not be enough to cover the damage the tenant has made.

Your Capital is at Risk: The value of your investment can rise or fall, as with any investment. However, if you do not keep up with the payments, you are at risk of losing your property. And, if you are in negative equity, that is, the value of your property is less than the loan, and your property is repossessed and sold by the bank, they may pursue you for any shortfall.

I explored different business opportunities, such as opening up a nursery school and investing in a range of assets such as stocks and shares, mutual funds, and commodities. And I even tried my hand at day trading, but none of them grabbed me like property.

Since I was a child playing Monopoly, I have always been passionate about property. While working, I followed my passion by creating a reliable and sustainable passive income for the long term. I knew deep down that one day, this would grow and become my main source of income and give me the option of quitting my job when I was ready.

It helps if you are passionate about the business. The thing about following your passion is that it doesn't feel like hard work. If you find your passion and can make a good living out of something that you enjoy, then that is the perfect combination.

The goal is the path. Find your passion, something you are good at, and create a reliable and sustainable passive income for the long term. Once you have found your path, persevere and stay in your lane. Stick to what you know, enjoy, and are good at. You may have to try several paths before you find the right one.

The property market is slow and cyclical, which makes it more predictable and less volatile than other markets. When the property market was at the bottom, we traded up and bought a large multi-dwelling unit. We stretched ourselves as far as we could afford. As the market grew, we redeveloped and increased the number of apartments. I was conscious of not risking what we had, so I chose to fund this through our savings rather than debt. Over time, the business grew, and at some point, the passive income from our investment properties began to exceed our expenses.

My favourite subject at school was Economics, so naturally, I looked at property from this perspective and developed my own strategy based on economic cycles. Although no two property cycles are the same, and you cannot predict government intervention, all economic cycles share the same four phases, namely expansion, peak, contraction and trough. The property cycle is no different. Understanding the property cycle can give you an insight into developing your investment strategy, depending on your goal, personal circumstances and risk appetite.

Most people will have heard of the great depression of 1929 and may think this was the first time the world experienced a huge crash. The reality is there have been many boom-and-bust cycles in the last century and even before that. In truth, there will be many more in the future as they are a normal part of the functioning of the world economy.

A little-known fact is that one of the first recorded crashes was the Tulip Bubble of the 1630s, which gripped Holland. Extreme speculation saw tulip bulb prices skyrocket. Tulip bulbs were trading for the same price as a house in Amsterdam! Inevitably, the bubble burst, prices collapsed, and many investors went bust.

Understanding the economic cycle and applying it to the property market can help you make better investment decisions. Each of the four phases of the economic cycle is different and requires a different strategy.

The property sector is a large part of any modern economy. Therefore, it follows that the property cycle and the general economic cycle for any country will have a strong correlation. However, the property cycle is complex.

Firstly, there is a time lag between the general economic cycle and the property cycle. This means that when the general economy grows, the property market may still be flat or falling.

There is also a time lag between when a house is sold and when it is reported. It is not unusual for properties sold today to be reported 4-6 months later.

Secondly, the property market is regional. This means that large regional variations exist, and when you look at your region, it may be very different from the national average. Local factors such as job opportunities, transportation and schooling can make a huge difference.

Thirdly, the reason the property market is so complex is that there are a large number of variables affecting the demand and supply of properties. The demand for properties is a function of the state of the general economy, buyer confidence, interest rate levels, supply of credit, affordability of properties, population size, and speculation. The supply of properties is a function of the state of the economy, government policy, business confidence, and the number of new properties being planned and developed.

Lastly, residential property is emotional. It is completely natural for homeowners to become emotionally attached to their properties as it is such a large part of their lives. This is why investors need to understand the psychology of buyers and sellers during each phase of the property cycle. Investors who understand what is going on in the minds of buyers and sellers during each phase of the cycle will make better investment decisions.

The good news is that it's possible to become a successful investor if you have a well-thought-through strategy. No investment strategy can guarantee success; that is just the nature of investing, and anyone telling you differently is lying. But, if you have a strategy based on sound economic theory and data, you put yourself in a strong position compared to someone who invests speculatively or on pure emotion.

Do not underestimate the importance of buyer and seller psychology. The property cycle investment strategy is based on Warren Buffett's famous quote, 'Be fearful when others are greedy, and be greedy when others are fearful.'

Property Cycle Investment Strategy

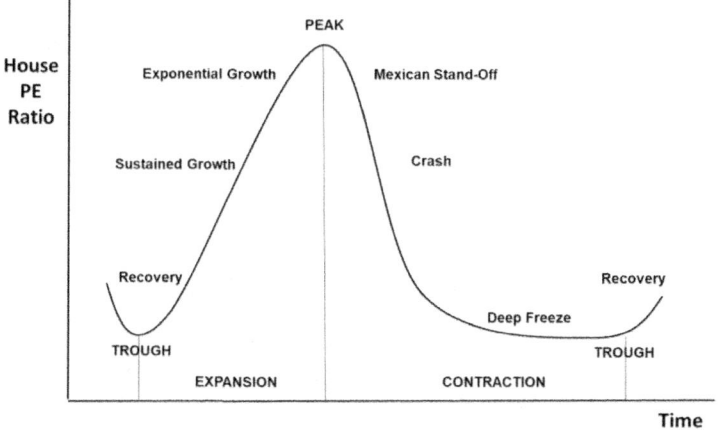

Let's run through the strategy for each of the four stages of the property cycle.

1. EXPANSION

Recovery:

***With property, you lock in your profit on purchase,
so everything comes down to preparation,
timing and deal selection.***

The early part of the expansion phase begins with a recovery, where you see house prices beginning to rise. Viewings, mortgage applications and the volume of properties sold increase month-on-month. During the recovery, there are very few buyers and plenty of stock to choose from. This is a buyers' market.

One of the big tell-tale signs is media stories reporting the 'green shoots' of recovery. There is now a growing awareness of the property market improving, and we see savvy buyers and experienced investors entering the market.

The emerging emotion is one of hope that the recovery is real and optimism for the future. However, the general public is still very cautious and has not entered the market.

Investment Strategy BUY: From experience, the recovery part of the expansion phase is a good time to buy, as house prices are low and yields high. It is a buyer's market, as the predominant market emotion is fear. I like to see at least three consecutive month-on-month increases in the house price index before I buy. That way, I don't jump in too early and get suckered in by a false dawn!

Sustained Growth:

During the main part of the expansion phase, there are strong house price increases. Sales volumes increase, the time it takes to sell reduces, credit policy is loose, and confidence returns to the market. Buyers return to the market in their numbers, and we see competition amongst buyers increase. This is also a time when developers enter a building frenzy, hoping to meet the growing demand.

There is general awareness that the property market is healthy and growing. There are more positive stories than negative stories in the media. We begin to see strong demand from the general public and investors.

After a period of sustained growth, the emerging emotion is one of belief and excitement. There is a belief that it is time to commit to buying a home and a general belief that you cannot lose money investing in property. There is also excitement amongst investors; they are making good returns on their investments, and there is an unlimited pipeline of new opportunities and cheap credit on the horizon.

Investment Strategy DEVELOP or BUY: From experience, I have used this phase to develop new units and look at ways to improve yield rather than be tempted by greed to buy more properties and overextend my borrowings. My preference is to develop existing properties during the main growth phase.

This is still a good time to buy. I learned early on that cashflow was more important than capital gains. You need to target properties that produce a reliable and sustainable positive cashflow. The reason for this is if you have a negative cashflow, you will need to put money in from your pocket each month to keep afloat. Moreover, the bank can repossess your property if you do not keep up with your payments and fall into serious arrears. If your property is repossessed, the bank will dispose of it at a fire-sale price, and any shortfall between the proceeds and the outstanding loan can be recovered by pursuing the investor.

If the value of your property falls, you can continue trading as it will recover over the long run. This is why timing is so important to improve your chances of success. Make your investment decision based on positive cashflow, as you need to service the loan and not just the potential of capital gains. Any capital appreciation is, therefore, seen as a bonus.

Exponential Growth:

During the latter part of the expansion phase, there are very few good deals to be had, as prices are high and yields low. The numbers just don't add up!

The media report year-on-year double-digit price increases, falling affordability and how difficult it's becoming for first-time buyers to get onto the property ladder. There is an almost religious belief that house prices only go up in value, and you cannot possibly lose money in property. More and more money pours into the property market.

The supply side sees over-development in construction as developers try to keep up with the anticipated demand.

The emerging emotion in the latter part of the expansion phase is best described as euphoria as the market is whipped up into a frenzy.

Investment Strategy HOLD: From experience, I have used this time to continue holding onto my properties and paying down my debt.

2. PEAK

At the top of the property market, it is a sellers' market. For an investor looking to buy, this would be the worst time to buy as house prices are high and yields low.

At this phase of the property cycle, general inflation is rising and starting to embed into the economy. Confidence has been replaced with irrational exuberance, sales volumes are high, with properties selling as soon as they are listed, and house prices have reached new record highs. There is a house-buying frenzy, where buyers bid up prices through fear of missing out (FOMO). There is a shortage of stock, and the property cycle is entering bubble territory.

There are usually tell-tale signs to predict the top of the cycle. There are media stories of yet another small garage in a prime location selling for a record high price, and gazumping, where a buyer outbids another buyer whose offer has already been accepted, has become common.

Typically, the peak is preceded by some external trigger. This might take the form of government intervention, such as the removal of property tax breaks, central bank intervention to increase interest rates to curb inflation, or an external shock, such as a global financial market crash, pandemic or war. There will be a trigger point, which will be the catalyst for the collapse.

The predominant emotion at this stage of the property cycle is greed, and as Warren Buffett would say, 'Be fearful when others are greedy.'

Investment Strategy HOLD or SELL: At this phase of the property cycle, investors should pause and hold their properties and address their financial position so they have sufficient funds available to get through the impending contraction, the next phase of the property cycle.

As interest rates rise to curb inflation, loan payments will increase sharply. Cashflow will be key to surviving the next phase. If you cannot service your loan payments in the event of serious arrears, there is a risk that the bank will repossess your property and sell it to recover the loan. If there is any shortfall, the bank will pursue you for it.

If cashflow is poor, investors should consider selling as house prices are at their peak. Properties with the largest loans, lowest capital gain or negative cashflow should be prioritised. Investors should continue to hold onto properties that produce a strong positive cashflow.

As an investor, if you are in the market to sell, to get the best price, you need to sell at the peak of the property cycle. At the peak, it's a sellers' market; there will be more buyers than sellers and a shortage of stock. It is quite likely that you will get multiple offers and sell for well above the asking price. Investors looking to sell should do so before the market turns, as demand is fickle and can slip away quickly.

3. CONTRACTION

Property may be a good way to make money, but without a well-thought-through strategy, property is also an easy way to lose a lot of money.

Mexican stand-off:

The early part of the contraction phase sees a Mexican stand-off between buyers and sellers. The number of viewings drop, mortgage applications fall, sales volumes fall, and chains collapse as buyers pull out.

Sellers are in denial and still market their properties at unrealistic levels, last seen at the peak. Buyers, however, feel properties are unaffordable with high prices and interest rates rising. They become cautious and wait to see what will happen to house prices.

The tell-tale signs are media stories of any downturn reported as a 'blip' or a correction and industry experts talking the market up with predictions of a soft landing. Estate agents will, of course, talk the market up, but this is a bit like swimming against the tide.

Other strong tell-tale signs are news of estate agents going bust and a slowdown in construction.

The predominant feeling is one of complacency and denial. Sellers believe the market has paused and will soon resume its stratospheric growth; they have not yet fully processed the new reality that the market has changed and property prices have started to fall.

Investment Strategy HOLD or SELL: My preference is to hold if you can see through the contraction.

However, if you need to sell and have missed the peak, don't panic. You will still be able to sell your property. Firstly, you need to instruct a good local estate agent, I cannot stress this enough. They are worth their weight in gold at this juncture. Their job will be to get the best price for their client. Secondly, you need to be realistic with your valuation. This is the hardest part for sellers. They often think they will still get the same price properties were trading for at their peak. The sooner you realise this and set a realistic asking price, the better.

Setting an unrealistic asking price will only mean you will generate very little interest and will have to drop the price even more tomorrow. It is better to take a drop of 10% today than suffer a 20% drop tomorrow.

Crash:

During the main contraction phase, house prices fall monthly, credit policy tightens, and interest rates start rising. During a credit crunch, banks tighten lending, de-risk their balance sheets and build up their cash reserves. Buyers become more cautious and wait for prices to fall further. In this phase, viewings and mortgage applications fall, more and more chains fall through, mortgage arrears rise, repossessions increase, and there is general doom and gloom in the sector.

Stock levels increase as the number of new instructions vastly exceeds the number of sales. Investors begin to off-load properties as cashflows turn negative because of interest rate hikes. The number of repossessed properties entering the market increases. If house prices continue to fall, we will have a prolonged decline or a full-blown crash.

The predominant emotion is one of anxiety and panic. Buyers have become extremely cautious and prefer to wait and not commit to buying a property. Sellers keep reducing their prices, but there are still too few viewings. Sellers are anxious and realise their houses will not sell as easily as they thought, and they will have to accept a much lower price, perhaps a 20%+ fall from the peak.

The Mexican stand-off has been replaced by seller capitulation as panic sets in.

Investment Strategy BUILD YOUR FINANCES: My preference during the crash phase is to pause and build up a war chest for the next deal.

The contraction phase is usually the longest part of the cycle. Most people worry when there is a contraction or economic recession, they start playing it safe. Experienced investors, on the other hand, realise the property market is cyclical. Instead of panicking, experienced investors know they can make more money during a downturn than when the market is booming.

During the crash phase, experienced investors buy distressed properties directly from banks or through auctions. There are also opportunities for experienced investors to buy unsold new builds directly from developers at a discount. There will be very few buyers, so experienced investors who are cash-rich can pick up some great deals and lock in their profits.

I learned that sitting on your hands was one of the hardest things to do in this phase of the property cycle, but patience wins as we are not at the bottom yet.

Deep Freeze:

During the latter part of the contraction phase, the property market freezes over with very little activity in terms of buying, selling, or price movement. There are very few buyers around as most are cautious and have been frightened off by the nightmare stories they read in the media. There are a large number of properties on the market left unsold as confidence is low amongst buyers and sellers.

The predominant emotion at this phase is one of anger. Many homeowners and inexperienced investors have lost money and are angry with the government for allowing this to happen.

Investment Strategy RESEARCH: My preference during this phase is to carry out research, keep yourself current with market news, and start viewing and shortlisting properties to target. Create a watch list of properties you are interested in.

You will need to have your finances in place for the next phase, which is to buy at the bottom of the cycle.

4. TROUGH

At the bottom of the property cycle, it is a buyers' market. For an investor looking to buy, this would be the best time to buy as house prices are low and yields high.

At this phase of the property cycle, inflation is under control, confidence is low, sales volumes are low, stock is high, and house prices have levelled. It's a buyer's market; that is, there are more sellers than buyers.

The usual tell-tale signs to predict the bottom of the cycle are interest rates falling back to normal levels as inflation is back under control. Experienced investors are drawn back into the market as yields are now attractive due to lower prices.

Many homeowners will have lost their life's savings, seen their wealth diminish, and their retirement plans fade away. Many investors will have lost money and wished they had not bought.

The predominant emotion is fear, and as Warren Buffett would say, 'Be greedy when others are fearful.'

Investment Strategy BUY: My preference is to buy and buy big if you can afford it.

To get the best deals, you will have built up your finances during the preceding contraction phase. If you keep your research current, you can create a watch list of the properties you want to target. With cash built up during the contraction phase and funding in place, you will have positioned yourself in the best possible place to buy at the bottom of the cycle.

Financially savvy investors
are cash-rich at the bottom!

The optimal time to buy a property is at the bottom of the property cycle. This is the time to make 'cheeky offers.' At this point, stock levels are high; many have been on sale for a long time, and there are rich pickings to be had. You need to get out there and start viewing properties and put in offers 10-30% below the asking price, and if one of those is accepted, you will have locked in a great deal.

At some point, the property cycle will begin to repeat itself, and we begin to enter the expansion phase again.

Having a strategy and a plan in place is smart, but be wary; governments do strange things to stay in power.

Finally, nobody ever gets their timing completely right every time. But the good news is that you don't need to time things perfectly. Buying close to the bottom or selling close to the top is just fine.

Before moving on, just a couple of points to note when dealing with data:

Do not look at just one set of numbers: Data must be cross-checked against other sources to ensure it makes sense. For instance, I look at industry data such as house price indices and affordability, such as the House P/E ratio, which is the ratio of average house prices to average earnings. I cross-check these with gross domestic product, inflation and interest rates. Effectively, I am cross-checking the property cycle with the economic cycle.

General Trends: Look for general trends rather than individual data points to get a sense of the direction of movement for the property market. Do not get over-excited by one month's data. A positive monthly movement in house prices does not mean that the green shoots of recovery have arrived, as the media so often report. I also look at quarterly price movements, as well as monthly data, as these iron out the blips.

Quality: The quality of data that you rely upon is critical. There are many competing data providers, and the information can be inconsistent and confusing. I prefer to use a few tried and tested data sources that have broad coverage and are relatively free from volatility and vested interest.

Beware of analysis-paralysis: There are many sources of information, and sometimes they signal different messages. Try to stick to a few good-quality sources for data.

The devils in the detail: Data providers use different measures to report their numbers. For instance, there are three types of prices: asking, agreed upon, and final. Make sure you understand the data you are using so that you can interpret it correctly.

In conclusion, the Property Cycle Investment Strategy is an investment approach based on sound economic cycle theory and data. There are four phases to the property cycle, which pose different challenges for an investor. Investors should keep an eye on the current state of the economy and the phase of the property cycle in which we are currently in. By adopting different investment strategies for each phase of the property cycle, it is possible to invest successfully across the entire cycle.

The above list is not designed to be exhaustive, but to give an insight into the different types of income-generating assets. The goal is to build up a diversified portfolio which produces multiple independent passive income streams.

Diversification reduces risk. By diversifying into different asset types, not putting all your eggs in one basket, you reduce the risk of loss. The idea is that if one of your assets makes a loss, this can be offset by gains generated by the others.

Once your passive income is greater than your expenses, you will have reached *Financial Independence*. You no longer feel dependent on your employer for a paycheck.

Cashflow pattern for the Financial Independence milestone

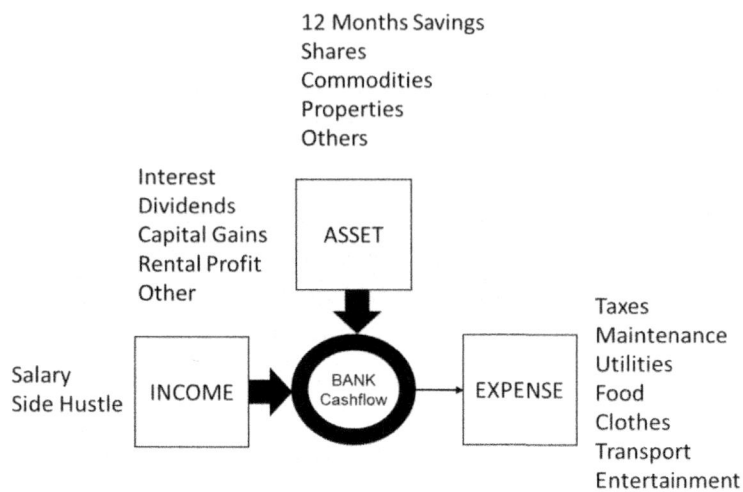

The KPIs for the Financial Independence milestone are:

Cashflow: You have a positive cashflow.

Savings Cover: You have 12+ months of expenses set aside as savings.

Short-Term Debt: You have cleared your short-term debt

Debt Free: You live debt-free.

Passive Income > Expenses: Your passive income > expenses.

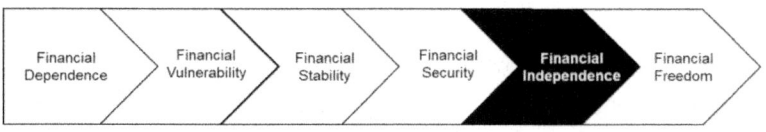

Now that you have achieved financial independence, there is only one question left: when do you get off the bus?

NOTES

CHAPTER 2.4:
Financial Freedom

Money is important as it gives you choices, and the best return on your money is to take back control of your time to live the life you want.

'Some people are so poor, all they have is money.'
- Bob Marley

S tage 4: Financial Freedom is categorised as Asset Rich - Time Rich. You will have left your job as your passive income covers the expenses for the lifestyle you want.

Financial freedom is a lifestyle choice. You choose how you want to spend your time, which is one of your most important resources. You can leave your job and live the life you want without having to worry about your next paycheck. You can choose the things you want to buy without feeling constrained by money. Financial freedom gives you the ability to live life on your terms.

All this is possible because you have managed your finances for the lifestyle you want.

The final milestone in the journey is Financial Freedom.

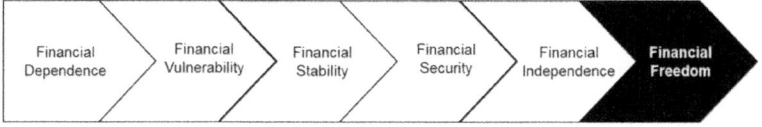

Cashflow pattern for the Financial Freedom Stage

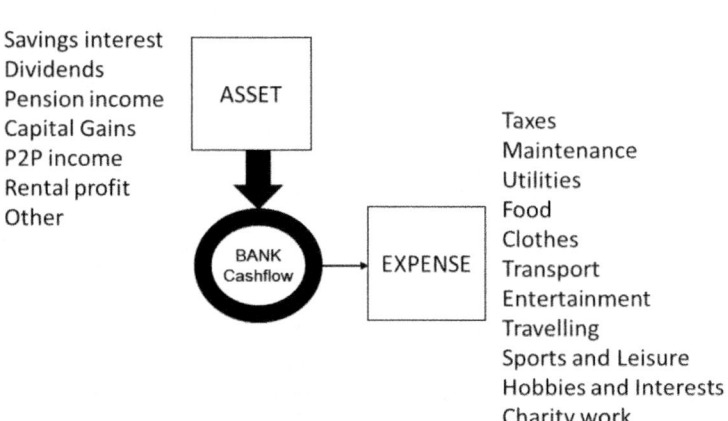

12-36 Months Savings
Stock Market
Pension Funds
Commodities
P2P Lending
Properties
Other

Savings interest
Dividends
Pension income
Capital Gains
P2P income
Rental profit
Other

ASSET

Taxes
Maintenance
Utilities
Food
Clothes
Transport
Entertainment
Travelling
Sports and Leisure
Hobbies and Interests
Charity work

BANK
Cashflow

EXPENSE

The KPIs for the Financial Freedom milestone are:

Cashflow: You have a positive cashflow.

Savings Cover: You have 12-36 months of expenses set aside as savings.

Short-Term Debt: You have cleared your short-term debt

Debt Free: You live debt-free.

Passive Income > Expenses: Your passive income > expenses.

From the outset, I want to note that not everyone will want to quit their job. Many people enjoy their jobs and have very fulfilling careers they get satisfaction from. If you are one of those fortunate people whose job is also their passion, then it makes perfect sense to continue working. There are also many people who go to work for social interaction rather than just the paycheck. If that is you, then continue working. If you need to work for financial reasons, then continue working. If your job makes you happy, continue working. Do what is right for you.

As a society, the narrative we have bought into is to go to school, get an education, get a job, work, and then retire at 65 years old on your savings and pension pot. This vision of the future is retiring at 65, spending your time, assuming good health, living a slower pace of life. Many of us have unconsciously bought into this social narrative, but it seems to me a strategy fraught with uncertainty.

When you are 20 years old and planning to work until 65, that is a long way off in the future. But life is not a straight line, and anything can happen between now and then. You or a loved one might have serious health issues, an accident resulting in a critical injury or, worse still, a fatal injury.

Sadly, I have had more than my fair share of close friends and family who have suffered such critical injuries and fatalities in the prime of their lives. These things are real and do happen.

A very close friend from university passed away at the age of 54 years old. I was devastated to hear the news as it was all very sudden. I had known him and his family for 30-plus years, and we went on many wonderful vacations together. He was a dentist with a thriving practice and worked incredibly hard all his life. He was still young, ran marathons, and was at the peak of his fitness. His best years were ahead of him, and sadly, those were taken away from him by a serious health issue. He worked hard all his life and even seemed to thrive under stress, but in the end, he did not enjoy the money he made.

Also, I hear many stories of people who work hard all their lives, and when they retire, within a short period of time, they pass away. They work so hard, but in the end, they never get to enjoy the money they make.

It seems that life is fragile. One minute, you are doing well, and the next, it can all disappear in the blink of an eye. This incident, and others, made me think about getting the balance right between work and life.

The other big factor was that I still wanted to do so much with my life, and as we age, some of those dreams seem to get further and further away. I had always been blessed with good physical health, but I knew if I left things too late, I might not be able to do many of the things I loved, such as travelling. Over time, our physical health naturally deteriorates. That's a fact. There are things I could do today that I will no longer be able to do ten years from now. So why wait? There was a balance to be had.

Before taking the leap to financial freedom, there are only two questions to ask yourself - Am I financially ready? And am I psychologically ready?

When calculating if you are financially ready, keep it simple. Do not fall into the trap of analysis-paralysis and overthink things by bringing too many variables into the equation. I have seen far too many people completely overanalyse things and, in the end, do nothing.

Keep it simple!

AM I FINANCIALLY READY?

Money gives you choices, and one of the biggest is the ability to leave your job and live the life you want. There are two parts to this question:

Do I have enough passive income to cover my expenses for the lifestyle I want?

The answer to what level of passive income you need to leave work is personal and will vary from individual to individual. However, what I can do is share my experience in the decision-making process.

If you want a simple lifestyle, you will need to build up a small passive income stream, and if you want a more comfortable lifestyle, you will need to build up a larger passive income stream. The phrase, 'You cut your coat according to your cloth,' best describes this situation. It means you make lifestyle plans and decisions based on the income you have. If you have a small amount of passive income, then you will have to accept making some sacrifices; otherwise, you will need to keep building up your passive income.

As a guide, in 2024, The Retirement Living Standards,[7] based on independent research by Loughborough University, developed a picture of what kind of standard of living we could have at different levels of income:

What standard of living can you expect					
Minimum		Moderate		Comfortable	
Single	Couple	Single	Couple	Single	Couple
£ 14,400	£ 22,400	£ 31,300	£ 43,100	£ 43,100	£ 59,000

Pensions and Lifetimes Savings Association (PLSA)

In much the same way, before I decided to leave my job in 2015, I carried out a 'bottom-up' approach to my regular monthly expenses and holiday costs to determine the minimum level of passive income required for the lifestyle I wanted. This included how much I would spend on food, home, utilities, transport, media, leisure, clothing and holidays. I also added a contingency of £100 pm to cover any unexpected costs.

Expenses	Monthly £	Annual £
Food	520	6,240
Home	414	4,968
Utilities	244	2,928
Transport	221	2,652
Media	94	1,128
Leisure	300	3,600
Clothing	160	1,920
Holidays	750	9,000
Contingency	100	1,200
Total Living Costs	**2,803**	**33,636**
Minimum Passive Income Required	**2,800**	**34,000**

This bottom-up exercise illustrated that we needed a passive income of about £34,000 pa in 2015 for the lifestyle we wanted. As our passive income already exceeded £34,000, this was a big tick in the box.

Around the same time, I recall a conversation with a senior colleague one late evening in the office. He looked preoccupied with punching numbers into a spreadsheet, and on the way back to my desk from the coffee machine, I popped over for a chat. After a short while, he showed me his spreadsheet, which projected his pension income if he retired at 60 or 65 years old. He was trying to work out whether to leave work and retire or continue working for another five years.

The projections he showed me were fairly modest, and I remember thinking to myself that I was earning that level of cashflow in my 40s from my passive income. This senior colleague was in his late 50s and always looked burned out and stressed to me. He had worked for the Bank all his life, yet the pension he projected to retire on was fairly modest. This was further affirmation that I was on the right path.

Do I have enough savings set aside as an emergency buffer?

The answer to what level of savings I should set aside as an emergency buffer will vary from individual to individual, as we all have different circumstances. This will be a combination of your known commitments, such as whether you plan on buying a new car, contributing towards your children's wedding cost or the deposit on their home, making any major repairs and renovations, and your risk profile.

As a rule of thumb, my experience showed that the emergency buffer, over and above your known commitments, should be somewhere between 1-3 years of annual expenses, depending on your circumstances. In the example above, that would be between approximately £34,000 and £102,000.

As I had put enough aside, this meant another big tick in the box.

In addition to carrying out this 'bottom-up' exercise, I asked some of my closest work colleagues and friends the same questions. I was surprised to hear how low their numbers were, suggesting that my calculations were conservative and a good rule of thumb.

AM I PSYCHOLOGICALLY READY?

'Freedom of choice is more to be treasured than any possession earth can give.' - David O. McKay

Once you have achieved your financial target, it becomes purely a psychological decision.

This is one of the toughest questions I had to ask myself. How do you know when you are psychologically ready to quit work? How do you know whether you are getting off the bus too early or have left it too late? Only you will know the answer to these questions, as it depends on your circumstances, but what I can do is share my experience in the decision-making process.

Some people will jump off at the earliest possible opportunity, whereas others may have a specific life event in mind. It could be a target age, or they want to see their children educated and settled.

For me, it was just a feeling. It felt like the right moment to leave work from a personal, family and career perspective. It felt like everything I had done in my life had got me to this point, and now all the stars were aligned. I was financially independent in my 40s, at which point I decided that I wanted to leave work at the target age of 50. If things did not work out, the only caveat was that under no circumstances would I work beyond 60. When I got to 50, this felt a little early, so I continued to work until the age of 53, when I decided I was psychologically ready.

Before that, my mother was poorly, and between the siblings, we took turns to provide care for her for two years. After she passed away, I never felt the same about work again. I was working for The Royal Bank of Scotland (RBS), and yet another round of cost-cutting and restructuring came, so I took redundancy. If I had not taken redundancy, I would have left anyway, as I felt all my stars were aligned, and now was the right moment for me. This was the final tick in the box; it was one of the easiest decisions of my life, and I have never looked back since.

From that moment onwards, all my big decisions have been about improving my quality of life. Most of what I have learned since quitting work can be summarised in one sentence:

> ***Money is important as it gives you choices and the best return on your money is to take back control of your time to live the life you want.***

The biggest 'bang for your buck' is not to buy luxury items such as an expensive car, yacht or holiday home but to gain control over your time.

We all have 24 hours in the day; however, the average person works for 8 hours, sleeps for 8 hours, travels to and from work for 2 hours, relaxes and watches TV for 2 hours, cooks, cleans and eats for 2 hours, which leaves about 2 hours a day to do all the things they enjoy.

You may ask, what about the weekend? Normally, one day is spent on entertainment and relaxation, and the other is spent catching up on all your chores.

> ***Having control of your time, the freedom of choice to do what you want, when you want is the pinnacle of wealth.***

My favourite time of day is just before I jump out of bed. I think through what I want to do and decide how to spend the rest of my day. I now understand that freedom of choice is priceless. You may decide to visit a museum, go to the theatre, have lunch at a fancy restaurant, meet up with a friend for coffee or a glass of wine, go to the beach or just go for a long walk along the river. The choices are countless. You are limited only by your imagination.

You are now your own boss; you no longer have someone to answer to and ask for permission. This freedom of choice is priceless.

Quality time is spending precious moments with the people you love doing what makes you happy. It's about creating experiences, making memories, enriching our lives and improving our relationships. Whether it's a family vacation or spending quality time together, these acts strengthen our bonds and bring joy.

For my 60th birthday, I treated my family, my cousins and their children to a holiday in the Canary Islands. I booked two adjoining apartments at Anfi Del Mar in Gran Canaria. We had the holiday of a lifetime. We relaxed by the pool, swam in the sea and enjoyed different water sports such as jet skis and paragliding. We ate, drank, sang, and danced together all week, and every day was full of belly laughs. This is what life is about spending quality time with the people you love.

'Time is more valuable than money. You can get more money, but you cannot get more time.' - Jim Rohn

Can money buy you time? The answer to this is yes and no.

Sadly, money cannot buy you *additional* time. There is a fixed number of hours in the day. The same is true for the length of your life. It is also true that you cannot get back a moment that has already passed.

However, *money can buy you quality time*. It gives you the ability to quit work earlier and live your dreams. Instead of working 8+ hours a day, you can spend your time doing things that make you happy.

Money can buy back time by freeing yourself up to do those things you enjoy. You can hire a gardener, a cleaner, or a builder, get your shopping delivered to your home and so on. All these time-saving options will allow you to buy back time by paying for convenience. Spending your money on convenience, especially if you have a busy lifestyle, is a luxury worth having. These conveniences save time and reduce stress, allowing you to spend time on things that truly matter.

If you are thinking, what will I do with my time? Will I get bored? This is fear talking; I have been busier since leaving work than I ever was before. Life is not boring, only boring people get bored. Use your imagination and follow your passion, as life is for living. I find it quite difficult to understand people who say they don't want to leave work because they do not know what to do with their time.

My whole life, I have been looking through the 'Money Lens', which measures wealth through material possessions. Chasing the big house, the flashy car, the swanky watch and as soon as you get them, the goalpost moves again, and you are chasing the next best thing, a holiday home, a yacht, and so on. The cycle never ends. The 'Money Lens' view of the world is that wealth is only financial. The more you have, the wealthier you are. This was quite a narrow view of the world.

I now realise that when you look through the 'Quality-of-Life Lens,' you see wealth as something far wider. You see wealth as having the freedom of choice to do what you want, when you want and for as long as you want. Freedom of choice is the pinnacle of wealth.

When you change your perspective and look through the 'Quality of Life' lens, you realise that having control over your time and freedom of choice is the ultimate currency.

Earlier, I said my preferred definition of financial wealth was being *debt-free* and having a *passive income that exceeds your expenses.*

However, true wealth is measured in terms of financial and non-financial wealth. How can you put a price on your freedom of choice to do what you want, when you want and for as long as you want? Freedom of choice is priceless.

True wealth is measured as:

Debt Free and Passive Income > Expenses (Asset Rich)
+
Freedom of Choice (Time Rich)

The point is, you can be financially wealthy but still poor, as you don't have the time and freedom of choice to do what you want when you want. I think this is what Bob Marley meant when he said, *'Some people are so poor, all they have is money.'* His richness came from life, not possessions.

The choices you make are personal, as each of us has our own idea of the lifestyle we want to live. Not everyone will want to quit work completely. Working part-time and using your time off to pursue your hobbies and interests can be a viable option. A close friend of mine works on the weekend, and on weekdays, he enjoys his life following his passion, and this brings him a lot of happiness. This freedom to choose what he wants to do makes him feel like the wealthiest man on the planet.

Alternatively, block working can also be an appealing option. A close work colleague works for two years as a freelance contractor and then takes a minimum of 6 months off for travelling.

I spend my time split roughly 20% managing my passive income, 20% travelling, 20% entertainment, 20% quality time with family and friends and the rest of my time is wasted playing golf!

As we get older, we acquire wisdom and look at things differently with the benefit of hindsight. In a survey published by the Nationwide Building Society Savings, people in their 70s were asked the question, 'If you could write a letter to yourself in the past, what would you tell yourself to do differently?' I find this question fascinating, as it asks elderly people what their biggest regrets in life were when looking back and what they would do differently.

Interestingly, none of them said they wished they had worked harder and had a bigger house or a faster car. The biggest regrets in life elderly people had were:

I wish I had travelled more

33% of those questioned regretted not having seen more of the world while they were young enough to do so.

Money gives you choices, but you need the courage to get off the bus, as this gives you the time to live the life you want without regrets later on.

I wish I had saved more money

31% said they had wished they had saved more money before retiring.

The survey also revealed that people in their 70s still had liabilities averaging £31,504, including mortgages, credit cards, personal loans, and overdrafts.

This is shocking but not surprising as our schools do not teach personal finance.

I wish I hadn't lost touch with a friend or a family member

17% of respondents said they lamented losing touch with someone close to them due to inattention or neglect.

I wish I hadn't lost a partner from the past

14% of those surveyed said they had romantic regrets from the past. They regret not voicing their unspoken thoughts to the 'one that got away.'

This is precisely why I am passionate about this subject. I want to live a life without regrets so that when you look back, you do so with a smile. I think the Italians say it best with the phrase, 'Live without regrets.'

Vivere Senza Rimpianti.

Looking back on our lives at any age can lead us to wish we had done things differently; perhaps we can take these findings as a reminder to live our lives without regrets.

What surveys like this reveal is that without exception, no one regrets not owning a bigger house or flashier car. Yet, we pursue these material possessions throughout our lives.

The main regrets involve missing out on experiences such as travelling, not saving enough money, falling into debt, not spending enough time with friends and family, worrying too much, not laughing enough and having the courage to live a life true to yourself and not the life others expected of you.

Whatever your age, ask yourself one question, 'If you could live a life without regrets, what would you change and do differently?' Do you want to look back at your life and have regrets, wondering what if, and wishing you had done things differently?

Life is for living; live life without regrets.

In addition to having hobbies and interests to pursue, it is also important to have a raison d'etre, a deeper purpose or reason for being. This is fundamental to being psychologically ready. This may be doing charity work, helping your family and friends, or helping people in need. This is something you should look forward to when you leave work and will act as a motivation for you. Having a purposeful life, a higher purpose, makes you feel good about yourself and a sense of giving back to your community.

In an earlier chapter, I mentioned that one of the pillars of my faith was selfless service. Charitable giving is a privilege. Charitable work and donations can bring a huge sense of fulfilment. It's about sharing, making a positive contribution to your community, and experiencing the joy of helping others and making a difference to their lives.

The next question is, how do you get from where you are today to where you want to be? That's the subject of the next chapter.

NOTES

CHAPTER 3:

Mind Your Own Business

How do you find balance?
Be patient, persistent, proactive, and resilient.

'If you want to make God laugh, tell him about your plans.'

– Woody Allen

Instead of making other people rich, for instance, your employer by giving them your labour, the banks by borrowing, the landlord by renting properties, and the government by paying taxes, start minding your own business and make yourself rich!

> **A financially savvy person manages their personal finances like a business.**

Mind your own business

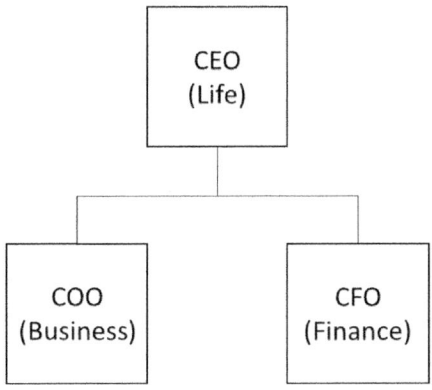

As the Chief Executive Officer (CEO), you are in charge of your life and must take responsibility for your actions. The buck stops with you. As the boss, you will need to wear two hats: the Chief Operating Officer (COO), responsible for minding your business and the Chief Financial Officer (CFO), responsible for minding your personal finances.

As COO, the first step on your journey to achieving your goal is to write up a game plan. A game plan gives you focus and clarity and will make you think about what steps are needed to achieve your goal. Planning helps focus the mind and energy towards your goal and improves your chances of achieving your dreams.

There are three main components to a game plan: a vision statement, a clearly defined goal and a plan of action.

Game Plan

A Vision Statement

All journeys begin in the mind. A vision is a dream, an idea or a picture in your mind of what the future looks like when you get there. You can crystallise your vision by articulating it in the form of a simple Vision Statement.

Writing it down makes it feel more real. Reading it out aloud to yourself keeps your dreams in sight and mind and gives you a better chance of making them come true.

When I was made redundant, with a baby on the way and a mortgage to pay, it was savage. I realised I was financially vulnerable and at risk of losing my home. This was a moment of clarity for me. I vowed never to be at the mercy of my employer or bank again, and from that moment onwards, my vision was to become financially free.

My vision statement was to have:

Financial Independence from my employer, so I would never be dependent on a paycheck.

Financial Security for my family so we could never lose the roof over our heads.

Control over my time, so that I could follow my passions like travelling, playing golf, making memories with my family and friends, and exploring new hobbies and interests such as cycling, tennis, cooking and charity work.

The vision statement has to be short; I would say, no more than a paragraph long, and high level, so not too detailed.

At this early stage, you should have a picture in your mind of the lifestyle you want to lead. In particular, what passions, hobbies, and interests you want to pursue.

In addition, it is important to have a purpose in life. This may be improving your mental, physical and spiritual health, voluntary work, helping your family and friends, and giving back to the community. This higher purpose gives meaning to your life.

A Clearly Defined Goal

The goal is your final destination. A clearly defined goal needs to be SMART, that is, Specific, Measurable, Agreed, Realistic and Timely. The goal helps give your vision, clarity and focus.

My vision was etched in my mind, but underlying this was a clear goal, which was defined as:

Specific: I want to achieve financial freedom.

Measurable: I want to

Live debt-free.
Save a minimum of three years of expenses.
Build up a passive income to afford a comfortable lifestyle.

Agreed: This was discussed and agreed with my partner.

Realistic: I felt the goal was achievable as I had a game plan.

Timely: My target age to achieve financial independence was 40 years old and financial freedom by 50. If things did not work out the way I planned, my plan B was to continue working until the maximum age of 60.

At the age of 43, I was financially independent, having paid off my debts and built up a passive income that exceeded my expenses. By the age of 53, I left work and achieved my dream of financial freedom.

Plan of Action

As COO for your business, you need to develop a plan of action (POA) to get you from where you are today to where you want to be. A plan is a roadmap to your final destination. The purpose of a plan is to set out a list of actions required to achieve your goal.

A good plan has the following characteristics, it is:

Comprehensive: The plan needs to address each major component of your finances – how to improve your income, how to reduce your expenses, what percentage of income to save, how to pay off your liabilities, which income-generating assets to acquire and your target passive income and savings.

Flexibility: There will be many bumps along the road, and not everything will go according to plan; therefore, it is important to monitor the plan and revise it if things go better or worse than expected.

For example, if your target age is 45 years old, but some investments performed worse than you expected, change the plan to 50 or leave work as planned but live a less extravagant lifestyle. You will always need a plan B, a backup plan.

Realistic: There is nothing worse than setting a goal that you know in the back of your mind is unachievable. A goal needs to be realistic, and at the same time, it needs to stretch you and take you out of your comfort zone.

Prudent: It is always better to underestimate your income and overstate your expense assumptions, and for prudence, add a contingency for any unknown expenses.

Life will throw things at you, and you, as a person, will change along the way. However, the vision needs to remain firm. *The plan can change, but the long-term vision remains the same.*

As everyone's journey is unique, you will have to balance the needs of yourself, your family and your work. Follow your path, and focus on what you want to achieve in your timescales. Do it on your terms, and don't try to copy others.

That doesn't work as their circumstances are different from yours.

For me, the most important word in the dictionary is *balance*. It is a bit like the circus five-plate balancing act, where each plate represents you, your family, your work, your health and your finances. You are constantly trying to keep all the plates up in the air. When you have managed to get all of the plates spinning, the first one begins to wobble and will need more attention, otherwise, it will fall and break. Your family and health will always come before anything else.

'There is only one way to eat an elephant, one bite at a time.' - Desmond Tutu

At times, we can feel overwhelmed by the task at hand, especially at the beginning, when things seem daunting. However, if you break down the goal into smaller, more manageable sub-goals and tackle them one at a time, it no longer looks daunting and will start to look achievable.

The financial freedom matrix has four distinct stages, each of which contains milestones. These are like significant landmarks along the journey, denoting progress towards your final destination. Your goal can be achieved by breaking down the final destination into six milestones. Then, in turn, each milestone is broken down into a list of sub-goals and actions.

Subgoals are smaller goals that need to be completed to reach your milestones. Actions are tasks that need to be completed to achieve your sub-goals. The idea is to break down the final destination into smaller, more manageable chunks and tackle them one at a time.

To illustrate how this works, I have used an example below. The financial freedom matrix provides a framework for this in columns 1, 2 and 3 below. You need to think about what actions are required to reach your sub-goals. Develop your list of actions with target dates in columns 4 and 5. I would suggest having a range of target dates as the plan is long-term. For instance, if you are financially vulnerable, you might want to give yourself 1-2 years to achieve financial stability.

Preparing a plan can be draining as you need to invest time thinking about what actions are required to achieve your overall goal, but once it's done, you will be pleased you have done it.

To help understand these planning terms, I like to use the analogy of a road trip:

> **Vision:** This is your *dream* of one day going on a road trip with your best friends.
> **Goal:** This is your *final destination* Z.
> **Plan:** This is the *roadmap* taking you from A to Z.
> **Milestones:** These are all the significant *landmarks* you will see along your journey.
> **Subgoals:** These are *smaller goals*, the towns and cities, B, C, D and so on, you will pass through on your journey.
> **Actions:** These are the detailed *tasks* you need to carry out, such as filling the car with fuel, taking the highway, driving for the next 2 hours and then taking the exit.

Not everyone will want to achieve full financial freedom in one step. Some are going to do it partially, while others will be content with just being in control of their finances by achieving financial stability. The advantage of this roadmap, is that it gives you the flexibility to adapt it to your personal circumstances and goals. So, let's look at someone who wants to achieve partial financial freedom to illustrate how to develop a vision statement, a clearly defined goal and a plan of action.

Let's take the example of a 26-year-old language teacher who we shall call Ms A. Ms A works as a full-time Spanish teacher at a secondary high school. Her vision is to work nine months a year as a freelance online language teacher and spend three months a year travelling in a camper van, all by the age of 40 years old.

Vision Statement: To quit my full-time job to work freelance and travel.

The Goal is defined as:
> *Specific*: I want to split my time between working nine months a year as a freelance language teacher and travelling three months a year in my camper van.
> *Measurable:*
>> Live debt-free.
>> £36,000 savings set aside as an emergency buffer equating to 1 year of expenses.
>> £10,000 pa passive income to pay for my lifestyle.
> *Agreed:* N/A as single.
> *Realistic:* The goal is realistic and achievable as I have a plan.
> *Timely:* Target age 40 years old.

Plan of Action: See below. Please note, the learner stage is not applicable as Ms A is already in the rat race.

FINANCIAL FREEDOM STAGE	KEY MILESTONE	SUB-GOALS	ACTIONS	TARGET DATE
1. Learner	Financial Dependence	Develop good habits when young	**Work ethic:** Develop a good work ethic by gaining work experience taking on weekend or summer jobs during college/university	N/A
			Living within your means: Develop habit of spending your money economically	N/A
			Save money: Develop habit of saving regularly	N/A
		Invest in yourself	**Education:** Go to college or university to learn Spanish and travel to a Spanish speaking country to practice your new skill	N/A
			Self-awareness: Understand your strengths and weaknesses, what you like and dislike, what you need and want	N/A
			Environment: Surround yourself with people who are positive and heading in the same direction as you	N/A
			Mentor: Find yourself a suitable mentor who can advise and guide you	N/A
2. Rat Race	Financial Vulnerability to Financial Stability	Increase your income	**Upskill:** Learn additional languages	
			More Hours: Consider working overtime, working towards that promotion or take on a second job	
			Side Hustle: Set up website and teach languages online and build up a side line business	
		Change your behaviour	**Collect data:** Go through your bank statement and split all regular monthly expenses between needs and wants	
			Eliminate any waste: Review direct debits, standing orders and cancel any subscription and memberships no longer required	
			Save money on needs: Review expenditure on big ticket items such as utilities and insurances to get the best deals	
			Reduce spending on wants: Review expenditure on any unnecessary purchases and cancel	
			S/T Debt: Pay off your short-term debt such as payday loans, credit cards, store cards, car loans, personal loans, overdrafts and 0% finance	
			Start building up your savings: Create a monthly budget allocating a percentage of your income to savings, needs and wants.	
			Emergency Buffer: Save 3 months of expenses as protection against unexpected bills or loss of income	
3. Investor	Financial Security	Pay off your LT Debts	**Live Debt Free:** Pay off all your long-term debts such as student loan and mortgage	
		Save 6 months of expenses	**Emergency Buffer:** Save 6 months of expenses as protection against unexpected bills or loss of income	
	Financial Independence	Buy income producing assets	**Invest in assets:** Consider additional savings, investing a small fraction of your salary each month in the stock market, investing in a rental property, making regular contributions to a pension fund, buying commodities for capital gains, peer to peer lending and other assets to generate a secondary income source	
4. Financial Freedom	Financial Freedom	Do I have enough passive income to cover my expenses	**Passive Income:** Have I reached my target passive income of £10,000 pa	
		Do I have enough savings set aside as an emergency buffer	**Emergency Buffer:** Have I reached my target of £36,000 savings	
		Am I psychologically ready	**Psychologically ready:** What is your gut saying ?	
		Quit your job	**Quit your Job:** Hand in my notice to leave my full time job and continue with on-line tutoring when I come back from travelling	
		Pursue the lifestyle you want	**Live the Life you want:** Buy a camper van, rent my home out when I travel for 3 months a year	

All plans need to be monitored periodically. I would suggest a long-term plan like this should be reviewed annually.

One of Mum's favourite sayings was, 'Work hard towards getting your golden egg, but don't forget to stop and have a few chocolate eggs along the way!'

The journey is just as important as the final destination. When you speed along the highway at 100 miles per hour, you miss all that natural beauty around you. You don't take in the scenery, the trees, the birds, the lakes, the sunrises, and the sunsets. Stop and get out of the car, enjoy the view, and take stock of your progress and accomplishments. Appreciate the distance you have travelled and what you have achieved. Enjoy the journey.

Don't forget to celebrate your achievements. Rewarding yourself along the way reinforces the progress you have made. Every time you reach a milestone, take a moment to stop and celebrate the progress you have made.

You learn so much about yourself, particularly your strengths and weaknesses. You discover talents you never knew you had.

As COO for your business, you have to take yourself out of your comfort zone. As a finance guy, I had very little experience in sales and marketing. As I built up my own rental business, the feedback I received from my customers was good, and this encouraged me to go it alone, as they preferred to deal with me rather than the letting agents I appointed.

My wife also encouraged me to manage the business independently. I ended up removing all my middlemen and bringing their roles in-house. I provided a full end-to-end rental service. I had no choice but to get out of my comfort zone and take responsibility for marketing, pricing, selling, negotiating, closing deals, writing up contracts, administration, collections, repairs and maintenance, dealing with third parties, meeting regulations, and so on. In fact, I found I was good at this and much better than most letting agents.

The ultimate goal was to believe in yourself.

The final destination may have been financial freedom, but I found the real hidden gem from this journey was believing in myself. I learned to overcome my self-doubts and began to trust myself. I learned to listen to experts but, in the final analysis, go with my gut instinct. I trusted my gut instinct and made decisions based on 70% gut and 30% numbers. That is, my gut instinct took priority over the numbers. This meant sometimes turning away opportunities and going for quality over speed.

I learned that if in doubt, say no and learn to walk away. For instance, when you are searching for new tenants, I find it is always better to wait for good-quality tenants rather than rush to minimise the void period. If your gut tells you there is something not quite right, then just walk away.

Playing it safe is one of the riskiest things you can do.

Playing it safe keeps you trapped in the rat race. We seek job security, but this is just an illusion. It was normal to go through restructuring or move every 2-5 years in my industry. In fact, in some banks where I worked, contractors were more secure than permanent staff.

I was not afraid to be unconventional and break from the herd. I learned to keep a positive attitude and not let negativity or fear control me. Work became a means to an end rather than an end in itself.

One of the most important lessons was to not panic and overreact impulsively to every new problem. By not reacting, you create space and time to respond from an emotional state of calm. By controlling your emotions and not being impulsive, you are more likely to make better decisions.

The ultimate goal was conquering your self-doubts, fears and negative thoughts and believing in yourself. It is these insecurities that keep us trapped in the rat race where you play it safe and seek security in a 9-5 job.

Now that we have a game plan, let's look at your job as the CFO for your finances.

NOTES

CHAPTER 4:
Financial Health Check

*Taking control of your finances starts
with being honest with yourself.*

*The 360 Cashflow Statement is a quick and
easy financial health check.*

W ho is in control? You, or your money?

Poor v Good cashflow patterns

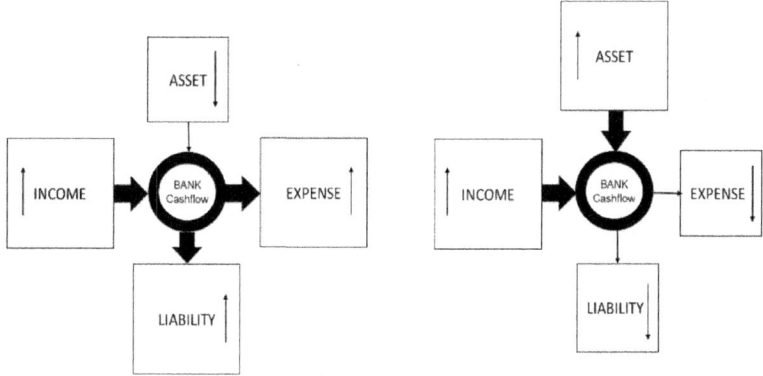

The cashflow pattern for someone who is not financially savvy is shown on the left-hand side. As their income rises, so do their expenses, a concept called lifestyle inflation. This is the classic middle-income debt trap, where making more money makes you poorer because you spend more and take on liabilities thinking you are buying assets!

Let's remind ourselves of the three biggest wealth killers: short-term debt, cars and homes, and why they are liabilities and not assets.

Short-Term Debts: Payday loans, credit cards, store cards, personal loans, overdrafts and 0% finance are liabilities because they take money out of your bank account through interest expense and fees.

Short-term debts are wealth killers because if you cannot pay off the balance in full, as and when due, the interest rate and fees charged are extremely high.

Car: A car you have bought outright is a depreciating liability, not an asset, as it takes money out of your bank account in the form of repairs and maintenance, taxes, insurance, fuel, roadworthiness tests and servicing costs.

Buying a car, a depreciating liability funded by a car loan on which you are paying interest is one of the biggest mistakes I see young people make. I understand why young people want a prestigious car in their 20s and 30s, but this is one of the biggest wealth destroyers.

This is a triple whammy. Firstly, you are taking on debt. Secondly, you pay the finance company interest on the car loan, and finally, the car depreciates year after year.

This is one of the fastest ways to destroy wealth and become poorer.

Home: A home is a liability.

To be more precise, a home is a necessary liability, as we all need somewhere to live.

Buying a home to live in is a liability, not an asset, because it takes money out of your bank account. There are expenses in the form of mortgage interest, building and contents insurance, utilities, repairs and maintenance to pay.

Even after the mortgage has been fully paid off, the home remains a liability as it still takes money out of your bank account.

Buying a home beyond your means is another wealth killer. Not only do you have to pay the mortgage, but the running costs, repairs, and maintenance can be quite substantial on a large property.

Contrary to what many people think, a home is not an asset. Any appreciation in value is an unrealised gain and, therefore, should be ignored from a cashflow perspective until it is realised. The way to realise any appreciation is to sell or re-mortgage. The problem with selling is that you still need somewhere to live. And, if you re-mortgage, you will now have acquired a liability on which you have to pay interest and repay the capital.

Many of us would like a nice watch, a luxury holiday, a prestigious car and a bigger home. That is not the issue here; the question is how we finance it. Debt destroys wealth, so the way to do it is with cash once you have built up your wealth.

The only exception to this is your home, where most of us don't have a choice but to take out a mortgage. However, once you have bought your home, try to pay down the mortgage as soon as possible.

This is how you obtain those luxury items. This involves a period of sacrifice, delayed gratification, when you are building your wealth. Once you can afford these items, buy them outright with cash instead of immediately with debt, which makes you poorer.

A financially savvy person knows to spend carefully even when their income rises. They make short-term sacrifices in favour of greater rewards in the future. Taking control of your finances sometimes means making tough decisions, like cutting out luxuries in the short term. This may seem restrictive at the time, but in the long run, it gives you something far more precious: financial freedom.

Financially savvy people put aside money as savings to create an emergency buffer, start paying off any debts and begin to invest in income-generating assets. The cashflow pattern for a financially savvy person is shown in the diagram on the right-hand side.

Beware of the credit score dilemma!

I want to briefly discuss credit scores. Credit scores measure your creditworthiness, that is, how worthy you are to receive new credit. Most lenders use these when making their lending decisions. The idea is to get a high credit score, which in turn gives you access to finance at cheaper rates. However, to get a high credit score, you need to have a credit history, which means you need to take out debt such as credit cards and personal loans. The credit score industry encourages people to get a higher credit score, which means taking out debt, but as we have learned, debt makes you poorer.

We want access to cheap credit, for instance, to buy your home, but you don't want to get poorer by taking on bad debt just to boost your credit score. This is the credit score dilemma!

My preference is to live debt-free, and if you live debt-free, you don't care about your credit score. As Mum always said, 'The best debt is no debt!'

The 360 Cashflow Statement is a quick and easy financial health check which you can carry out once a year.

The 360 Cashflow Statement is designed to help manage your money.

As CFO for your personal finances, you are responsible for managing your cashflow. Taking control of your finances starts with being honest with yourself. Completing the 360 Cashflow Statement will provide you with an overview of your finances. This is done by completing the boxes with details of your income, expenses, assets and liabilities.

The 360 Cashflow Statement provides:

A 'one-page' snapshot of your current financial status.

An overview of your cashflow pattern: you can see how your money comes in and goes out.

A summary of the 5 KPIs to determine which milestone you have reached.

A monitoring tool used to measure and track your progress towards your goal.

The table below summarises the relationship between the 5 KPIs and the milestones, and by completing the 360 cashflow statement, you can determine which milestone you have reached. Note that the milestones are sequential; that is, you cannot move to the next milestone without the criteria for the preceding ones being complete.

KPI/Milestone table

#	KPI's	Criteria	Learner	Rat Race			Investor		Financial Freedom
			Financial Dependence	Financial Vulnerability	Financial Stability		Financial Security	Financial Independence	Financial Freedom
1	Cashflow	Do you have a positive cashflow ?	N/A	N	Y	Y	Y	Y	Y
2	Savings Cover	How many months of expenses have been set aside as savings ?	N/A	< 3	3 +		6 +	12 +	12-36
3	Short-Term Debt	Have you cleared all your Short-Term Debt ?	N/A	N	Y		Y	Y	Y
4	Debt Free	Are you living debt free ?	N/A	N	N		Y	Y	Y
5	PI > EXP	Does your passive income exceed your expenses ?	N/A	N	N		N	Y	Y

360 Cashflow Statement

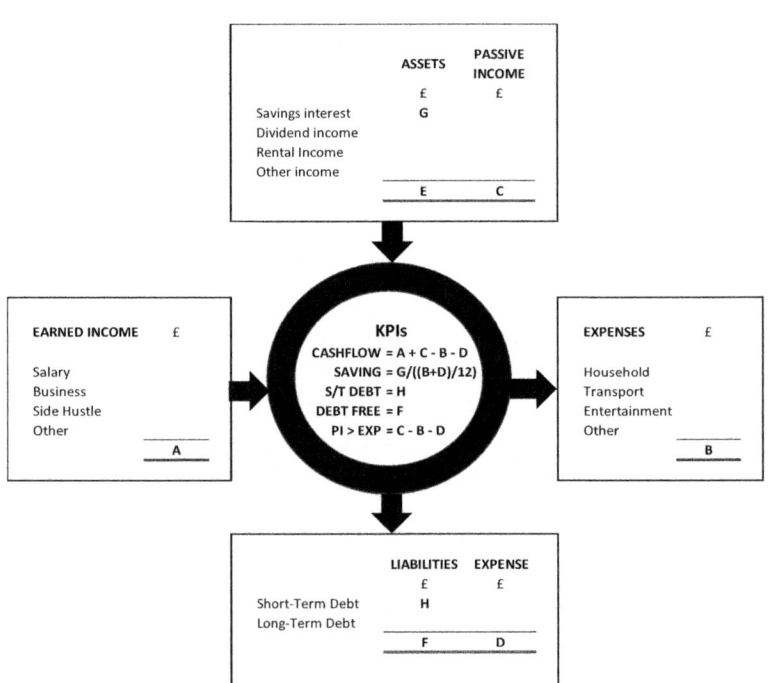

The 5 Key Performance Indicators (KPIs) are:

1. Cashflow: Do you have a positive cashflow? A positive cashflow builds wealth because you have more money coming in than going out. A positive cashflow occurs when your total income is greater than your total expenses, that is, Total Income (A+C) > Total Expenses (B+D).

2. Savings Cover: How many months of expenses have been set aside as savings? This measures the size of the emergency buffer, our cushion against short-term cashflow shocks arising from unexpected bills or a loss of income. This is calculated as Savings (G) / Average Monthly Expenses((B+D)/12), or simply put as Total Savings/Average Monthly Expenses. The aim is to have between 3-12 months covered while you are working and 1-3 years covered after you quit work.

3. Short-Term Debt: Have you cleared all your short-term debt? This measures our dependency on bad debt. The aim is to pay off all your bad debt, such as payday loans, credit cards, overdrafts, store cards, car loans, personal loans, 0% finance, etc. This occurs when Short-Term Debt (H) = 0.

4. Debt Free: Are you living debt-free? This measures what we owe. The aim is to pay off your long-term debt (student loan and mortgage) and live debt-free. This occurs when Liabilities (F) = 0.

5. Passive Income > Expenses: Does your passive income exceed your expenses? This is a measure of financial wealth. This is calculated as Passive Income (C) > Total Expenses (B+D).

You are independently wealthy when you meet all 5 KPIs.

Notes:

a) Income is after-tax pa and expenses are pa.

b) Savings includes all current and savings account balances.

c) If the credit card balance is cleared in full each month, then treat this as a nil balance.

d) Long-term debt comprises student loans and mortgage; all other debt is short-term debt.

e) For investment properties: disclose the loan balance under asset or liability, depending on whether the net cashflow is positive or negative (if fully redeemed, show a nil balance together with any associated income or expense).

f) For your home: disclose any outstanding mortgage as a liability, with household expenses shown separately in the expense box.

This is best illustrated with an example: let's take a typical 30-year-old, who we shall refer to as Mr B.

Mr B works as a retail manager and owns his own apartment. After years of working, he feels like he is not getting anywhere. He feels trapped in the rat race; whatever money comes in goes out again, and is relying on his credit card to supplement his income. He is not financially savvy, and although he has a good salary, he lives paycheck to paycheck.

Mr B completes a 360 Cashflow Statement at the end of year 1. This shows that Mr B has a salary of £31,000 from his job with total expenses of £36,000 (Expenses £30,000 + £6,000). Mr B has a negative cash outflow of £5,000 (Total Income £31,000 - Total Expenses £36,000). Mr B spends more than he earns, so he supplements his income by putting £5,000 on his credit card.

Year 1: According to the table, Mr B's KPIs fall into the *Financial Vulnerability* milestone:

Cashflow = -£5,000: You don't have a positive cashflow.
Savings Cover = 0: You have < 3 months of expenses set aside as savings.
Short-Term Debt = £5,000: You haven't cleared your short-term debt such as payday loans, credit cards, overdrafts, store cards, car loans, personal loans, 0% finance etc.
Debt Free = £105,000: You do not live debt-free.
Passive Income > Expenses = -£36,000: Your passive income < expenses.

Whatever money comes in goes out again. Mr B is just about managing.

Mr B has left himself financially vulnerable. He has no savings to fall back on. If there is an unexpected bill, such as a parking fine, he will go further into debt. Moreover, if he loses his job, becomes critically ill or is involved in a serious accident, he is at risk of losing his home if he doesn't keep up with the mortgage payments.

360 Cashflow Statement at the end of Year 1
Financial Vulnerability

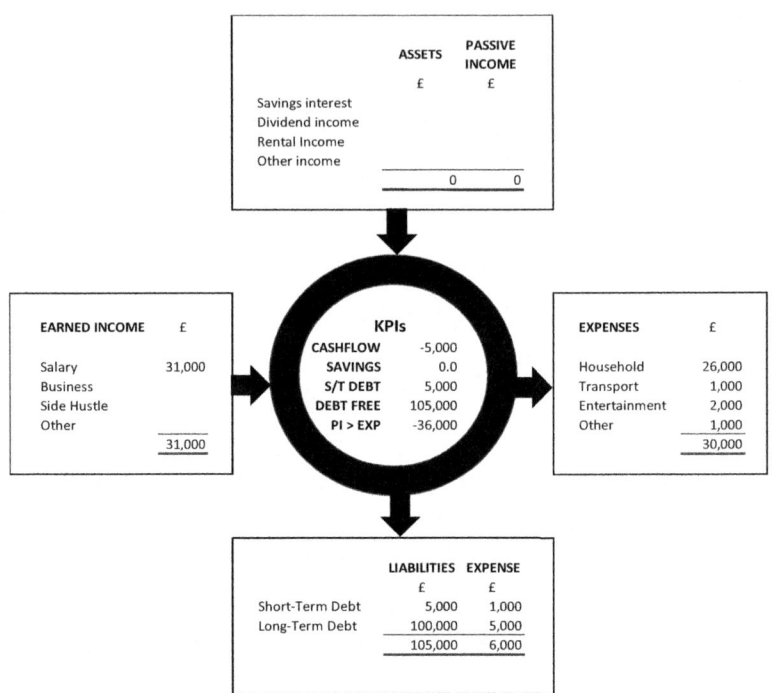

The 5 KPIs are:

Cashflow = - £5000

This is calculated as Income (£31,000 + £0) - Expenses (£30,000 + £6,000) = -£5,000

Savings Cover = 0

This is calculated as Savings £0/ Average Monthly Expenses ((£30,000 + £6,000)/12) = Nil

Short-Term Debt = £5,000 outstanding

Debt Free = £105,000 liabilities outstanding

Passive Income > Expenses = -£36,000 shortfall

This is calculated as Passive Income £0 - Expenses (£30,000 + £6,000) = -£36,000

After completing a 360 Cashflow Statement at the end of year 1, he realises he must do something about this. Mr B decides to take control of his finances and begin his journey to financial stability. He increases his earned income by working overtime and making additional money selling items online as a side hustle. In addition, he begins to cut back his spending, and with the money left over each month, he pays off his credit card and begins to build up his emergency buffer.

At the end of year 2, Mr B decides to complete another 360 Cashflow Statement to see how he has done. Mr B has earned a total income of £40,000 pa (Salary £34,000 + Side Hustle £5,000 + Savings Interest £1,000). His total expenses were £27,000 pa (Expenses £22,000 + £5,000).

Mr B now has a positive cashflow of £13,000 pa (Total Income £40,000 - Total Expenses £27,000). This was used to pay off his credit card debts by £5,000 and put aside £8,000 as savings by the end of the year.

Year 2: According to the table, Mr B's KPIs now fall into the *Financial Stability* milestone:

Cashflow = £13,000: You have a positive cashflow.
Savings Cover = 3.6x: You have 3+ months of expenses set aside as savings.
Short-Term Debt = £0: You have cleared your short-term debt.
Debt Free = £100,000: You do not live debt-free.
Passive Income > Expenses = -£26,000: Your passive income < expenses.

360 Cashflow Statement at the end of Year 2
Financial Stability

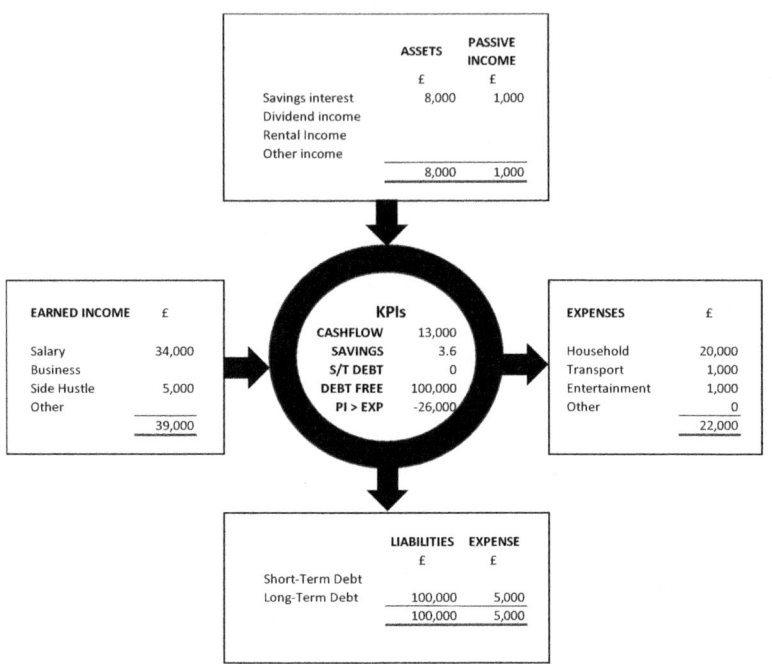

The 5 KPIs are:

Cashflow = £13,000
This is calculated as Income (£39,000 + £1,000) - Expenses (£22,000 + £5,000) = £13,000

Savings Cover = 3.6x
This is calculated as Savings £8,000/ Average Monthly Expenses ((£22,000 + £5,000)/12) = 3.6x

Short-Term Debt = £0

Debt Free = £100,000 liabilities outstanding

Passive Income > Expenses = -£26,000 shortfall
This is calculated as Passive Income £1,000 - Expenses (£22,000 + £5,000) = -£26,000

We can conclude that Mr B has improved his financial health by moving from *Financial Vulnerability*, living paycheck to paycheck, to *Financial Stability* within a year. Mr B is now in control of his finances, and not vice versa.

Before we finish, let's take a look at the biggest obstacle to success - Yourself!

NOTES

CHAPTER 5:

Believe in Yourself

Stop copying others, be yourself,
as everyone else is taken.

You are getting in the way of yourself.

S elf-doubt is a feeling of having no confidence in your abilities and decisions. It's that inner voice that tells us we are not good enough, nothing ever good happens to us and that we are going to fail.

The truth is we all have self-doubts and feel insecure every now and then, especially when we do something challenging outside of our comfort zone. However, if these feelings persist, self-doubt can become crippling. It can hold you back from following your dreams and reaching your full potential. You lose confidence and start letting opportunities pass you by. You begin to procrastinate, and you start finding excuses for not doing things. The main obstacle to success is yourself.

Fear allows self-doubt to creep in. This could be fear of failure, making mistakes, losing money or fear of what other people might be thinking. Fear makes you stay in your comfort zone and stifles personal growth.

Playing it safe is the worst place to be. You have a choice: to stick with the herd and feel safe in the rat race or break from the herd and follow your path. The unconventional path is never easy, but the prize is financial freedom.

So how do you overcome self-doubt? I learned through playing sports that success is not just based on natural talent, hard work, and practice; a large part of success is mental. To win in sports, you must believe in yourself and battle that inner voice. It's about taking control of your thoughts and actions and erasing any self-doubts that creep into your mind by believing in yourself.

Think about self-doubt as negative thoughts and feelings that creep into your mind. We need to counter these with some positive thoughts and feelings that kick self-doubt into the touchline. Let me share some techniques I learned through playing sports, which I still practice today to stay positive and erase self-doubt as soon as I feel it.

Surround yourself with positive people

The people we surround ourselves with can have a huge impact on our mindset.

We all have self-doubts, but what doesn't help is having people around us giving negative vibes all the time. These people often say things like: If it is such a good idea, how come no one else has done it yet? What if it doesn't work out? Or that will never work!

Avoid these doom-mongers and naysayers. Their negative talk will drag your spirit down. Confidence can be a fragile thing, and these words will chip away at your confidence and allow self-doubt to creep back in.

In contrast, when you surround yourself with positive people, their positivity rubs off. Positive people will boost your self-confidence and help keep self-doubt in check. Seek out people who are positive and bring out the best in you.

Positive people inspire, motivate and boost your confidence. When you surround yourself with people who are positive and believe in themselves, some of their magic rubs off on you.

Visualise success

This is a technique I use to counter thoughts of failure when I am facing challenging situations. Visualising success prepares you mentally for a positive outcome. Before putting any major decision into action, I visualise what success looks like. This helps me to focus on succeeding and stopping any negative feelings creeping in.

The opposite is also true. If you visualise failure, then it can become a self-fulfilling prophecy.

If you are facing a challenging situation, visualise the last time you succeeded in a similar situation and see those self-doubts fade away.

Positive self-talk

Words are powerful. What we tell ourselves has a huge impact on our mindset and, in turn, how we feel about ourselves and our actions.

We all have negative thoughts enter our mind from time to time, and if these persist, they can hold us back from pursuing our dreams.

I use positive self-talk proactively to counter these negative thoughts. For instance, I praise myself and reflect on any successes I have had to boost my self-confidence.

Negative thoughts are a bit like having a little red devil on your left shoulder, whispering negative messages in your ear. I counter this with positive self-talk, which is like having a little white angel on my right shoulder whispering positive messages in the other ear.

Positive self-talk can have a huge impact on your self-confidence and be a powerful shield against self-doubt.

Small wins

Goals need to stretch you and take you out of your comfort zone, but they also need to be realistic and achievable. There is nothing worse than setting unrealistic goals. If you set the bar unrealistically high, you set yourself up for failure, which in turn can damage your self-confidence.

Sometimes, we can feel overwhelmed by the task at hand, especially at the beginning, when things seem daunting. However, if you break down the overall goal into smaller, more manageable chunks and tackle them one at a time, it no longer seems overwhelming.

Achieving small wins helps motivate, build momentum and boost confidence. These small wins will counter any negative thoughts and feelings arising from self-doubt, and you will watch those negative thoughts fade away.

Self-awareness

Being self-aware of your thoughts and feelings is a form of emotional intelligence. Being mindful of how you are feeling and reacting enables you to recognise self-doubt when it creeps into your mind.

Being self-aware of your negative thoughts enables you to remove yourself from the situation and become an observer of your thoughts rather than get swept away by them. If you can remain level-headed, gather your thoughts, adjust, and deal with any situation from a calm place, you will make better decisions.

One of the most important lessons for me was not to panic and overreact to every new problem. By not immediately reacting, you create space and time to respond from an emotional state of calm and not panic. By controlling your emotions, you are more likely to make better decisions.

Most problems are not as big as we imagine and are fixable. By creating this space and coming back to the problem after a few hours, you find your mind has stopped racing away and is in a much calmer place to resolve the issue.

See failure as an opportunity to learn and grow

Failing at something new or outside your comfort zone is perfectly normal and not a sign of being weak or incompetent. In fact, failing is a normal part of personal development and growth. At school, I failed my fair share of exams and even dropped a year to retake some papers. Failure never stopped me from persevering and passing with better grades the second time around.

Failure has a way of feeding your self-doubt. The fear of failing can paralyse you into doing nothing, but once you see failure as a learning and growth opportunity, the hold that self-doubt has on you begins to fade away.

In business, no one ever wins 100% of the time. At some point, you will lose money. You just have to accept that this is part of the game. In reality, you never really lose as you learn from your experience and take that forward.

I very rarely get things right the first time; in fact, it takes me, on average, about three attempts to get things right. What is more important is how you deal with failure. It is your ability to get up, dust yourself down and carry on that really matters. Your ability to bounce back after a setback distinguishes you from the herd. The key is to persevere and not give up on your dreams.

Fear of failure or losing money can make you play it too safe, and this is far worse. It is true that you can lose money by taking risks, but you can also lose money by playing it too safe. If you take no risk, then you are forgoing investment opportunities by letting the fear of losing hold you back.

It is far better to take a calculated risk than no risk. Rather than play it safe and miss out on opportunities, learn to manage risk. Start small; that way, you limit the amount you may lose, and as you gain experience and confidence, you can invest more, diversify, and build up your assets one step at a time.

Celebrate your achievements

When we focus too much on our failures and mistakes, we allow self-doubt to creep in. However, if we change our focus to what we have achieved, this completely changes our mindset. Celebrating our achievements is a way of acknowledging and reinforcing our accomplishments, and this is a powerful way to counter any self-doubts.

The final destination may have been financial freedom, but the real hidden gem was the journey and learning to believe in yourself.

Thank you for reading this book, I hope it was helpful. I would really love it if you would leave an online review on the site where you purchased the book.

NOTES

CHAPTER 6:
Overview

Do not give your children money;
give them something far more important:
The knowledge to make, keep and grow money.

This section provides a summary of the salient points from each chapter and can be used as an aide-memoire for those who need a quick refresher.

But before we do that, I want to share a story about a little bird.

One day, a little bird was happily singing and flying home before winter set in. All of a sudden, the weather changed for the worse. It turned so cold the bird's wings froze, and it fell to earth in a field covered in snow. Later that day, a cow was passing by. It saw our bird and dropped a heap of dung on it. The dung covered our bird, and the warmth thawed the snow and the bird's wings. The bird felt warm and happy and started singing out loudly again. A friendly cat heard the bird singing and came to investigate. Following the sound, the cat discovered the dung and opened it up to help set the bird free. The bird thanked the cat for his help, but just as the bird was about to fly, the cat pounced and ate up our little bird.

The moral of the story is:

> Even when things are going well, challenges can come along anytime and bring you back to earth with a bump.

> There are good people out there who are prepared to help you, such as your parents, teachers, good friends, and mentors. Seek out the company of positive people and those who are moving in the same direction as yourself.

> There are also bad people out there who will befriend you only to use you for their own ends. Pick your friends wisely. You do not need too many friends, just a few good ones.

> When you are warm, comfortable, and doing well, keep your mouth shut!

Introduction

- Financial freedom is a lifestyle choice.

You choose how you want to spend your time, which is one of your most valuable resources. You can leave your job and live the life you want without having to worry about your next paycheck. You can choose the things you want to buy without feeling constrained by money.

Financial freedom gives you the ability to live life on your terms. All this is possible because you have managed your finances for the lifestyle you want.

- The journey to financial freedom begins with an underlying desire.

- Your darkest hour can transform an underlying desire into a burning desire.

- An education and a well-paid job don't offer financial security.

- If you want to become independently wealthy, you need three key attributes: ability, desire and application.

Ability: Financial literacy gives you the ability to be in control of your finances and not the other way around. In particular, understanding cashflow patterns gives you the knowledge to manage your finances and make decisions that build wealth.

Desire: A burning desire is normally triggered by a life-changing event, which can transform an underlying desire into a burning desire.

Application: All journeys begin in the mind. A vision is a dream, an idea or a picture in your mind of what the future looks like when you get there, and this can be realised through having a game plan.

The key attributes to becoming wealthy

- This means anyone, regardless of income level, can become wealthy. Building wealth has more to do with your mindset and behaviour than your ability to earn more income.

Chapter 1: Financial Literacy

- Financial literacy is the cornerstone of building wealth. Before we start building wealth, we need to build our financial knowledge.

- Financial knowledge enables you to understand the pattern of cashflows. Being financially literate helps you to manage your money in a way that builds wealth.

- The Cashflow Model is a summary of all the cash movements flowing in and out of your bank account.

The Cashflow Model

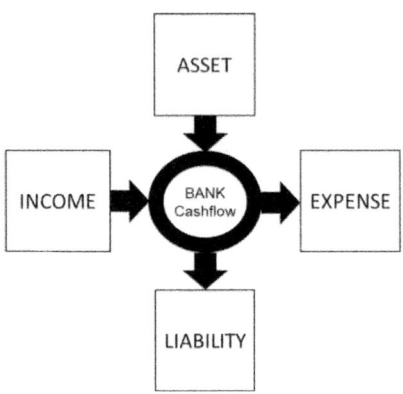

The term cashflow refers to the net amount of cash flowing in and out of the bank account, therefore, cashflow can be positive or negative. A positive cashflow arises when the cash flowing in exceeds the cash flowing out of the bank account. Conversely, a negative cashflow arises when the cash flowing out exceeds the cash flowing in.

The cashflow definition of income, expense, asset and liability are:

INCOME: A transaction that puts **money into** your bank account.

EXPENSE: A transaction that takes **money out** of your bank account.

ASSET: Something you own or are owed that puts **money into** your bank account.

LIABILITY: Something you own or owe that takes **money out** of your bank account.

- Good cashflow management creates wealth, and poor cashflow management destroys wealth.

Low and middle-income vs wealthy cashflow pattern

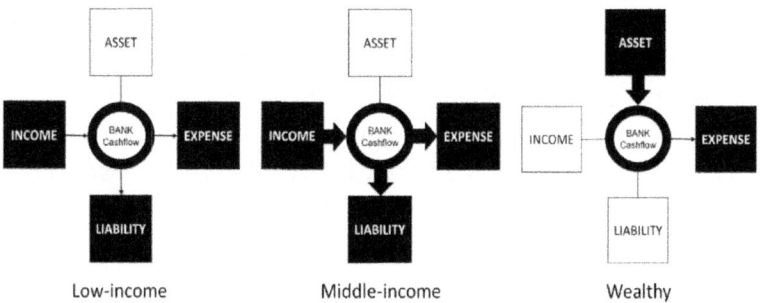

Low-income   Middle-income   Wealthy

- Many low and middle-income families are just about managing to stay afloat. Their cashflow pattern shows whatever money comes into the bank as earned income goes back out again in the form of expenses and debt interest.

- On the other hand, the cashflow pattern for the wealthy shows they have assets that generate a passive income in the form of interest, capital gains, dividends, rental income, and so on, which covers their expenses and any surplus is then re-invested to buy more assets, so their wealth continues to grow.

- You are independently wealthy when you live debt-free and your passive income exceeds your expenses.

- Financial knowledge gives you the power to make better-informed decisions and avoid costly mistakes.

Chapter 2: Financial Freedom Matrix

- There are four stages in the Financial Freedom Matrix, but there are many ways to get there.

Learner: This is categorised as Asset Poor - Time Rich.
Rat Race: This is categorised as Asset Poor - Time Poor.
Investor: This is categorised as Asset Rich - Time Poor.
Financial Freedom: This is categorised as Asset Rich - Time Rich.

The Financial Freedom Matrix

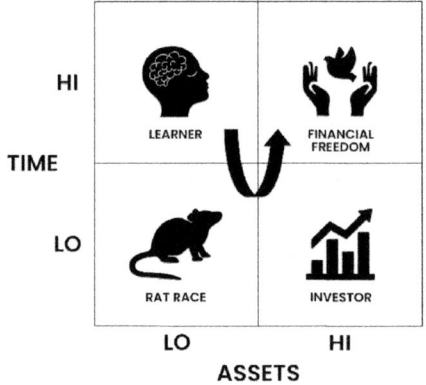

- The Financial Freedom Matrix is a roadmap. Each stage has corresponding milestones, as shown below, from which you can develop a your own plan to help achieve your goal.

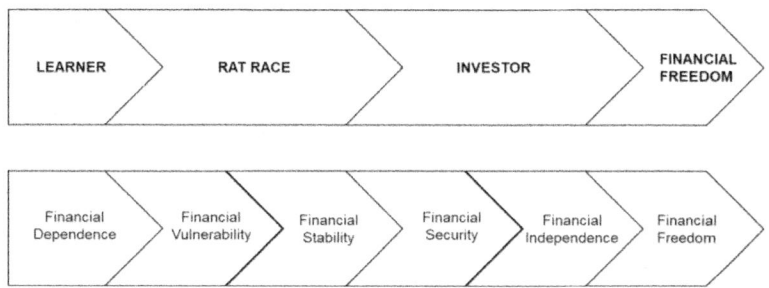

- Everyone's journey is unique. Follow your journey, but do it in a way that balances the needs of yourself, your family, your work and your health.

- Enjoy the journey; what you learn, how you overcome challenges, and how you grow and develop are just as important as the final destination.

Chapter 2.1: The Learner

- Stage 1: The Learner is categorised as Asset Poor-Time Rich.

Cashflow pattern for the Learner Stage

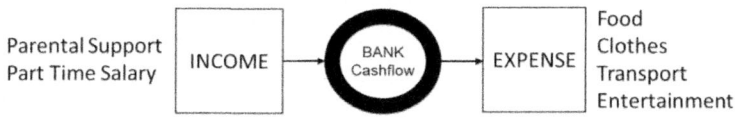

This diagram shows the cashflow pattern for a typical 18-year-old student living at home and working part-time. Their income would be parental support and a small salary from their part-time job. Their expenses are mostly necessities like food, clothing, transport and entertainment.

The *Financial Dependence* milestone describes a situation where you are financially dependent on your parents for necessities like food, clothes and a roof over your head. This is why the KPIs are N/A for this milestone.

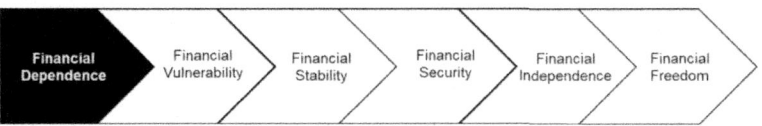

- The actions during the Learner Stage are:

Behaviour: Parents should encourage their children to develop behaviours that encourage them to become independent, such as building a strong work ethic, spending money carefully, and regularly putting some money aside for savings. These behaviours will become habits that remain with your child for the rest of their life.

Games and Sport: Playing games and sports are a great way for young people to learn new skills. Specific games and sports like Monopoly, Chess and Golf help you to learn how to manage your money, think strategically and build mental strength and discipline.

Education: Your biggest income-generating asset is your brain. Education is one of the best investments you can make. You must believe in yourself and back yourself. Education and upskilling can open doors and increase your income-earning potential.

Self-Awareness: As a young adult, take time to reflect and understand yourself, your strengths and weaknesses, what you like and dislike, and what you need and want from life. Self-awareness, which is a form of emotional intelligence, can help direct you to a career path that matches your character and one in which you are more likely to be successful. Self-awareness as a soft skill can benefit you in the workplace by helping you manage time, stress, people, and career progression.

Environment: Pick your friends carefully. Surround yourself with positive people who are heading in the same direction as you.

Mentor: Find a mentor who is approachable, listens to you, understands what you want, and above all, is experienced and successful in the subject matter. They can offer invaluable advice and help when you are young and lack experience.

Chapter 2.2: The Rat Race

Stage 2: The Rat Race is categorised as Asset Poor-Time Poor.

Typically, you will have completed your formal education and are now working or running your own business.

You wake up, go to work, pay the bills and go to bed ... the next day, you wake up, and the cycle continues. This is the rat race, an endless, self-defeating, pointless pursuit. Whatever money comes in goes out again, and by the end of the month, you have nothing to show for all your hard work. You feel like you are working hard only to make your employer, the government, the banks and the landlord rich!

This is potentially one of the longest stages, ranging from 20 to 65 years old. Most people remain trapped in the rat race until they retire in their mid-60s unless they have a plan B, a backup plan.

During the rat race stage, you move from *Financial Vulnerability* to *Financial Stability*.

This can be achieved by increasing your income, and perhaps more significantly for most people, by changing your behaviour.

Cashflow pattern for low and middle-income families

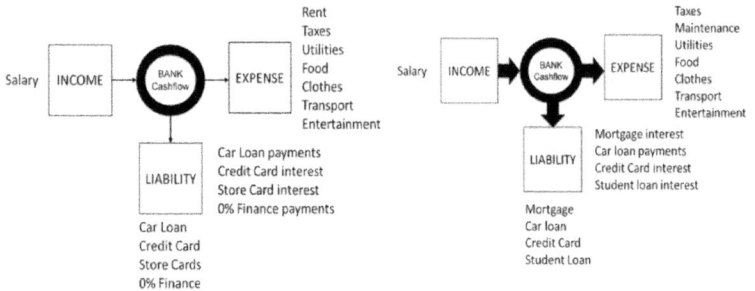

Many low and middle-income families live paycheck to paycheck, with very little savings held as an emergency fund. This state is called *Financial Vulnerability*. These families live on a knife edge and are just one or two paychecks away from going broke.

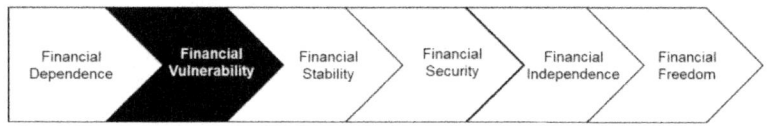

The KPIs for the Financial Vulnerability milestone are:

Cashflow: You don't have a positive cashflow, or
Savings Cover: You have < 3 mths of expenses set aside as savings, or
Short-Term Debt: You haven't cleared your short-term debt, such as payday loans, credit cards, overdrafts, store cards, car loans, personal loans, 0% finance, etc.
Debt Free: You do not live debt-free.
Passive Income > Expenses: Your passive income < expenses.

- For those who feel trapped in the Rat Race, there are two main actions required to move from *Financial Vulnerability* to *Financial Stability*:

> *Increase your income:* The best way to increase your income is by working more hours, upskilling through investing in yourself, or starting a profitable side hustle.
>
> *Change your behaviour:* Follow the **Six Steps to Saving:**
>
> 1. Collect Data.
> 2. Eliminate any waste.
> 3. Save money on needs.
> 4. Reduce spending on wants.
> 5. Pay off your short-term debts.
> 6. Start building up your savings by setting aside a *minimum* of 10% of your take home pay.

- Mum's 1/3rd rule … 1/3 Saving,1/3 Needs & 1/3 Wants.

Mum's 1/3rd rule is simple to understand and implement. As a rule of thumb, you pay yourself first, and then the balance is split equally between your needs and wants.

If you live at home saving 1/3rd is achievable, if not, then there are no hard and fast rules about how much to set aside as savings each month, as it depends on your personal circumstances and how quickly you want to achieve financial independence. ***Nevertheless, as a minimum you should set aside at least 10% of your take-home pay, and split the balance between your needs and wants, according to your personal circumstances.*** The important point is, you are building up your savings, and the more you can save the quicker you will reach your goals.

Cashflow pattern for the Financial Stability milestone

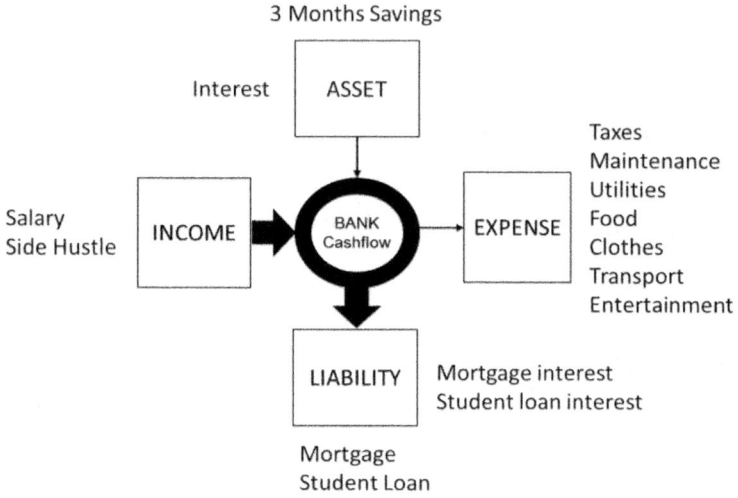

If successful, at this point you will have transitioned from *Financial Vulnerability* to *Financial Stability*. You now feel in control of your money and not the other way around. You have managed to control your spending habits, paid off your short-term debt, and set aside enough money as an emergency buffer to cover any unexpected bills or expenses for a few months if you were to lose your job.

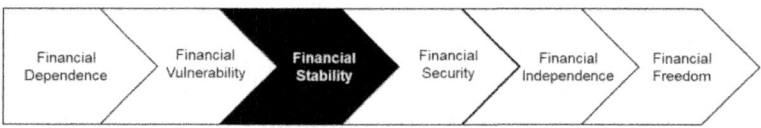

The KPIs for the Financial Stability milestone are:

Cashflow: You have a positive cashflow.

Savings Cover: You have 3+ months of expenses set aside as savings.

Short-Term Debt: You have cleared your short-term debt

Debt Free: You do not live debt-free.
Passive Income > Expenses: Your passive income < expenses.

Chapter 2.3: The Investor

Stage 3: The Investor is categorised as Asset Rich - Time Poor.

Typically, you are in full-time employment, developing your side hustle, striving to live debt-free, and generating a passive income stream by acquiring assets. Over time, your passive income will grow and become a greater proportion of your total income. You are growing less and less dependent on your paycheck.

During the investor stage, you are transitioning from:

Financial Stability to Financial Security by living debt-free, and from
Financial Security to Financial Independence by buying income-generating assets.

Cashflow pattern for the Financial Security milestone

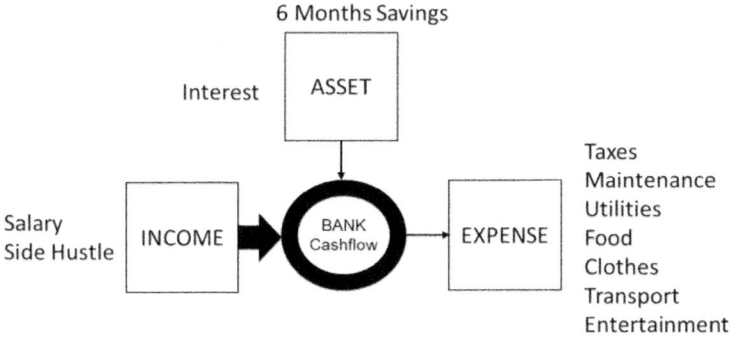

I define *Financial Security* for my family as living debt-free so you can't lose the roof over your head. To achieve financial security, the main actions are to build up your savings to six months of expenses and pay off your long-term debt, such as your student loan and mortgage.

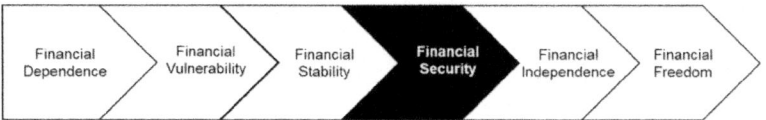

The KPIs for the Financial Security milestone are:

Cashflow: You have a positive cashflow.
Savings Cover: You have 6+ months of expenses set aside as savings.
Short-Term Debt: You have cleared your short-term debt
Debt Free: You live debt-free.
Passive Income > Expenses: Your passive income < expenses

- It is a myth to say that passive income requires no effort.

- Passive income can be generated from savings, stock market investments, pension funds, commodities, peer-to-peer lending, rental income, royalties etc.

- Quality earnings meet the following criteria:

Reliable: The cashflow comes in regular month-on-month.
Sustainable: The cashflow will continue in the long run
Robust: The underlying business model is strong and will always be in demand.
Inflation proof: The cashflow will increase over time.
Effort to reward ratio: Low effort - High reward.

Cashflow pattern for the Financial Independence milestone

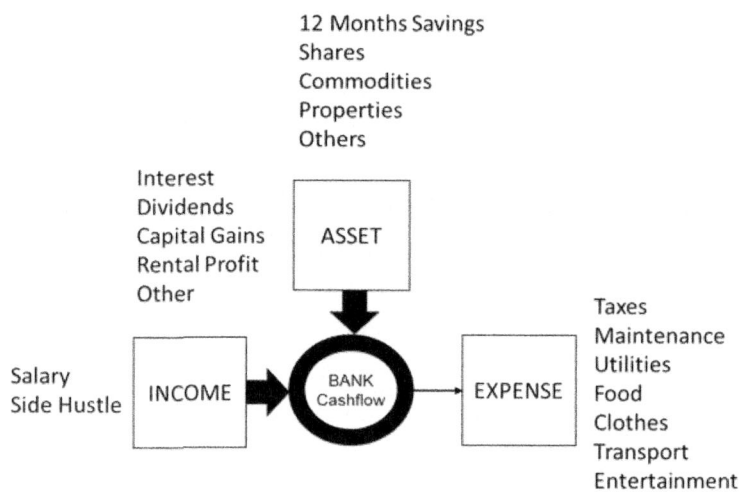

I define financial independence as not being dependent on an employer for a paycheck. To achieve financial independence, the main actions are to build up your savings to a minimum of twelve months of expenses and to buy income-generating assets. When your passive income exceeds your expenses, you will achieve financial independence.

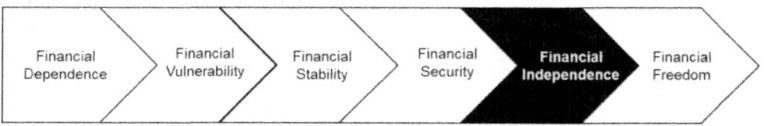

The KPIs for the Financial Independence milestone are:

Cashflow: You have a positive cashflow.

Savings Cover: You have 12+ months of expenses set aside as savings.

Short-Term Debt: You have cleared your short-term debt

Debt Free: You live debt-free.

Passive Income > Expenses: Your passive income > expenses.

Chapter 2.4: Financial Freedom

Stage 4: Financial Freedom is categorised as Asset Rich - Time Rich.

Financial freedom is a lifestyle choice. You choose how you want to spend your time, which is one of your most valuable resources. You can leave your job and live the life you want without having to worry about your next paycheck. You can choose the things you want to buy without feeling constrained by money. Financial freedom gives you the ability to live life on your terms.

All this is possible because you have managed your finances for the lifestyle you want.

Cashflow Pattern for the Financial Freedom Stage

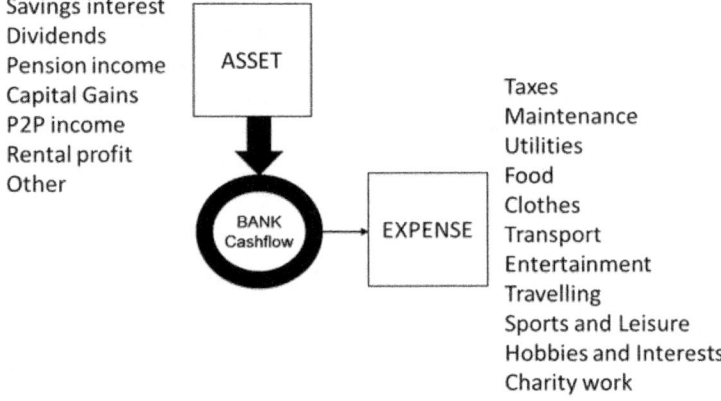

12-36 Months Savings
Stock Market
Pension Funds
Commodities
P2P Lending
Properties
Other

Savings interest
Dividends
Pension income
Capital Gains
P2P income
Rental profit
Other

ASSET

Taxes
Maintenance
Utilities
Food
Clothes

BANK
Cashflow

EXPENSE

Transport
Entertainment
Travelling
Sports and Leisure
Hobbies and Interests
Charity work

- Once you have managed your finances to live the life you want, the key action during this stage is deciding when to get off the bus.

- Avoid analysis-paralysis by keeping it simple. There are only two questions to ask yourself:

Am I financially ready?

Am I psychologically ready?

If you have ticked both these boxes, it's time to get off the bus!

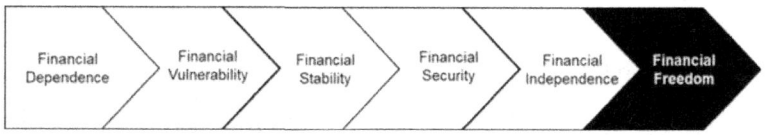

The KPIs for the Financial Freedom milestone are:

Cashflow: You have a positive cashflow.
Savings Cover: You have 12-36 months of expenses set aside as savings.
Short-Term Debt: You have cleared your short-term debt
Debt Free: You live debt-free.
Passive Income > Expenses: Your passive income > expenses.

- Money gives you choices, and the best return on your money is to take back control of your time so that you can live the life you want.

- True wealth is measured in terms of financial and non-financial wealth. Having control of your time, and the freedom of choice to do what you want, when you want is the pinnacle of wealth.

- True wealth is measured as:

Debt Free and Passive Income > Expenses
(Asset Rich)
+
Freedom of Choice
(Time Rich)

Chapter 3: Mind Your Own Business

- There are three main components to a game plan: a vision statement, a clearly defined goal and a plan of action.

A *Vision Statement* describes what the future looks like when you get there.

A *Goal* is the final destination. A clearly defined goal is one that is Specific, Measurable, Agreed, Realistic and Timely (SMART).

A *Plan Of Action* is a list of actions to get you from where you are to where you want to be.

Chapter 4: Financial Health Check

- The cashflow pattern for someone who is not financially savvy and who lives paycheck to paycheck is shown on the left-hand side. As their income rises, so do their expenses. This is the classic middle-income debt trap, where making more money makes you poorer because you take on liabilities thinking you are buying assets!

Poor v Good Cashflow Management Patterns

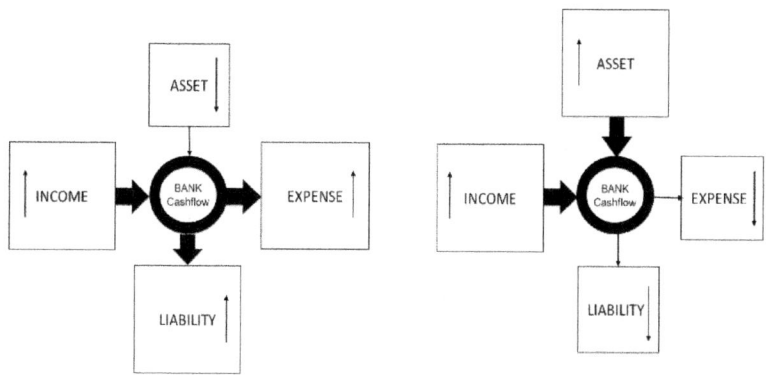

- As their incomes rise, financially savvy people put aside money as savings to create an emergency buffer, start paying off any debts, and begin to invest in income-generating assets. The cashflow pattern for a financially savvy person is shown in the diagram on the right-hand side.

- The 360 Cashflow Statement is a quick and easy financial health check and provides:

A 'one-page' snapshot of your current financial status.

An overview of your cashflow pattern: you can see how your money comes in and goes out.

A summary of the 5 KPIs to determine which milestone you have reached.

A monitoring tool used to measure and track your progress towards your goal.

360 Cashflow Statement

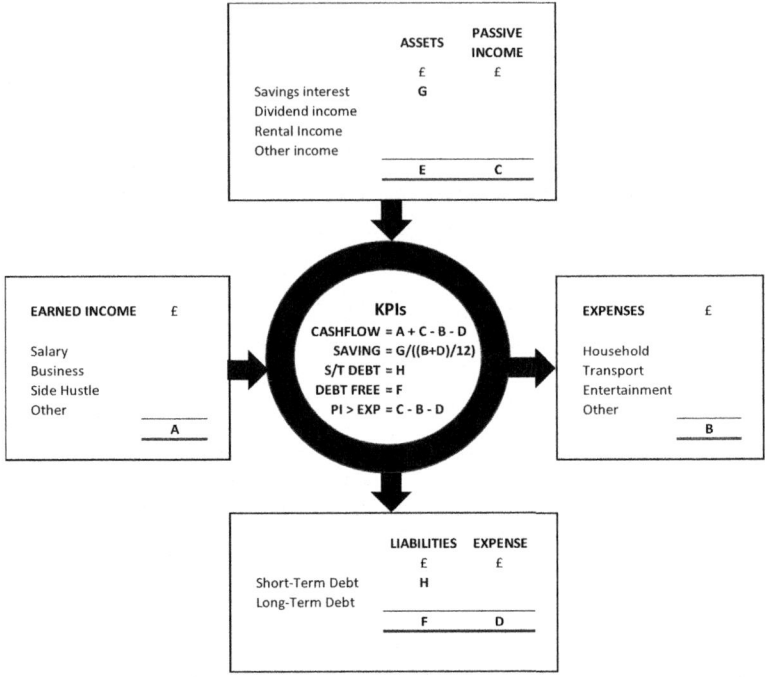

- The 5 Key Performance Indicators (KPIs) are:

1. Cashflow: Do you have a positive cashflow? A positive cashflow builds wealth because you have more money coming in than going out. A positive cashflow occurs when your total income is greater than your total expenses, that is, Total Income (A+C) > Total Expenses (B+D).

2. Savings Cover: How many months of expenses have been set aside as savings? This measures the size of the emergency buffer, our cushion against short-term cashflow shocks arising from unexpected bills or a loss of income. This is calculated as Savings (G) / Average Monthly Expenses((B+D)/12), or simply put as Total Savings/Average Monthly Expenses. The aim is to have between 3-12 months covered while you are working and 1-3 years covered after you quit work.

3. Short-Term Debt: Have you cleared all your short-term debt? This measures our dependency on bad debt. The aim is to pay off all your bad debt, such as payday loans, credit cards, overdrafts, store cards, car loans, personal loans, 0% finance, etc. This occurs when Short-Term Debt (H) = 0.

4. Debt Free: Are you living debt-free? This measures what we owe. The aim is to pay off your long-term debt (student loan and mortgage) and live debt-free. This occurs when Liabilities (F) = 0.

5. Passive Income > Expenses: Does your passive income exceed your expenses? This is a measure of financial wealth. This is calculated as Passive Income (C) > Total Expenses (B+D).

You are independently wealthy when you meet all 5 KPIs.

- The table below summarises the relationship between the 5 KPIs and the milestones, and by completing the 360 cashflow statement, you can determine which milestone you have reached. Note that the milestones are sequential. That is, you cannot move to the next milestone without the criteria for the preceding ones being complete.

KPI/Milestone table

#	KPI's	Criteria	Learner	Rat Race			Investor		Financial Freedom
			Financial Dependence	Financial Vulnerability	Financial Stability		Financial Security	Financial Independence	Financial Freedom
1	Cashflow	Do you have a positive cashflow ?	N/A	N	Y	Y	Y	Y	Y
2	Savings Cover	How many months of expenses have been set aside as savings ?	N/A	< 3	3 +	6 +	12 +	12-36	
3	Short-Term Debt	Have you cleared all your Short-Term Debt ?	N/A	N	Y	Y	Y	Y	Y
4	Debt Free	Are you living debt free ?	N/A	N	N	Y	Y	Y	Y
5	PI > EXP	Does your passive income exceed your expenses ?	N/A	N	N	N	Y	Y	Y

Chapter 5: Believe in Yourself

- Self-doubt is a feeling of having no confidence in your abilities and decisions. It is that inner voice that tells us that you are not good enough, that nothing ever good happens to you and that you are going to fail.

- The truth is we all have self-doubts and feel insecure every now and then, especially when we do something new and challenging outside of our comfort zone. However, if these feelings persist, self-doubt can become crippling. It can hold you back from following your dreams and reaching your full potential. You lose confidence and start letting opportunities pass you by. You begin to procrastinate, and you start finding excuses for not doing things. The main obstacle to success becomes yourself.

- The main ways to counter self-doubt are to surround yourself with positive people, visualise what success looks like, positive self-talk, small wins, develop self-awareness, see failure as an opportunity to learn and grow and celebrate your achievements.

- Believe in yourself.

References

1. Sportskeeda, 'How much money did Mike Tyson earn per fight on average,' (2022).

https://www.sportskeeda.com/pro-boxing/mike-tyson-average-fight-purse

2. Maria Montessori, 'The Absorbent Mind,' p266 (1995).

3. The Resolution Foundation, 'Precautionary Tales: Tackling the problem of low saving among UK households,' (12 February 2024). https://www.resolutionfoundation.org/publications/precautionary-tales

4. The Automobile Association, 'Car Buying: Car Depreciation – Find out how quickly new cars lose money,' (23 March 2012). https://www.theaa.com/car-buying/depreciation

5. Which?, 'How do Mortgage Payments Work?' (2 November 2022). https://www.which.co.uk/money/mortgages-and-property/mortgages/remortgaging-and-managing-your-mortgage/how-do-mortgage-payments-work-aKbpA2H4Pcwn

6. Trade that swing, historical average stock market returns for S&P 500. https://tradethatswing.com/average-historical-stock-market-returns-for-sp-500-5-year-up-to-150-year-averages/

7. Pensions and Lifetimes Savings Association, 'Retirement Living Standards' (2024). https://www.retirementlivingstandards.org.uk

Acknowledgements

There are many people I would love to thank for their encouragement and support in writing this book. However, there isn't enough space on this page to list them all, so I am going to mention a few who have been particularly supportive throughout my journey:

I want to thank my dearest wife, **Bonny** and lovely son, **Amman**, for their feedback, creativity, continuous support, and positive vibes.

Raminder Atwal, for providing incisive and detailed constructive feedback.

Kiran Champion, for her creative input and ideas.

Dr. Arjun Saggu for his comprehensive review and challenge, suggestions for improvement, and unwavering genuine encouragement and support.

John Demello and **Kenneth Lau** for being my sounding board and providing valuable feedback.

Last, but certainly not least, I want to thank my economics school teacher, dear **Mr. Clopet**, and the many talented staff at Elthorne Park High School for inspiring me to aim high.

Visit the Rat Race to Riches website to find useful resources to save you TIME and EFFORT, and help put your plan into action!

Access the 360 Cashflow Statement, a quick and easy **FINANCIAL HEALTH CHECK** that provides:

A 'one-page' snapshot of your current financial status.

An overview of your cashflow pattern: you can see how your money comes in and goes out.

A summary of the 5 KPIs to determine which milestone you have reached.

A monitoring tool used to measure and track progress towards your goal.

Plus, lots of other helpful resources to get you started.

www.ratrace2riches.com

Printed in Great Britain
by Amazon

60666029R00129